W9-APS-092

Women Explorers

Mary Kingsley
Explorer of the Congo

Women Explorers

Women
Explorers

Mary Kingsley
Explorer of the Congo

Heather Lehr Wagner

Introduction: Milbry Polk,
author of *Women of Discovery*

CHELSEA HOUSE
PUBLISHERS
A Haights Cross Communications Company
Philadelphia

CHELSEA HOUSE PUBLISHERS
VP, NEW PRODUCT DEVELOPMENT Sally Cheney
DIRECTOR OF PRODUCTION Kim Shinners
CREATIVE MANAGER Takeshi Takahashi
MANUFACTURING MANAGER Diann Grasse

Staff for MARY KINGSLEY
ASSOCIATE EDITOR Kate Sullivan
PRODUCTION EDITOR Megan Emery
SERIES & COVER DESIGNER Terry Mallon
LAYOUT 21st Century Publishing and Communications, Inc.

©2004 by Chelsea House Publishers,
a subsidiary of Haights Cross Communications.
All rights reserved. Printed and bound in the United States of America.

A Haights Cross Communications Company

http://www.chelseahouse.com

First Printing

9 8 7 6 5 4 3 2 1

Library of Congress Cataloging-in-Publication Data

Wagner, Heather Lehr.
  Mary Kingsley : explorer of the Congo / by Heather Lehr Wagner.
    v. cm. — (Women explorers)
  Contents: A new destination — Life behind the shutters — A feeling of
responsibility — Studying the destination — At home in Africa — Navigating the Ogoou River — A new lake and a new river — A distant
land.
  ISBN 0-7910-7714-4
  1. Kingsley, Mary Henrietta, 1862-1900—Juvenile literature. 2. Women
explorers—Africa, West—Biography—Juvenile literature. 3. Women
explorers—Congo River Valley—Biography—Juvenile literature. 4.
Women explorers—Great Britain—Biography—Juvenile literature. 5.
Explorers—Africa, West—Biography—Juvenile literature. 6. Explorers—Congo River Valley—Biography—Juvenile literature. 7. Explorers—Great Britain—Biography—Juvenile literature. 8. Africa,
West—Discovery and exploration—British—Juvenile literature. 9.
Congo River Valley—Discovery and exploration—British—Juvenile lit-
erature. [1. Kingsley, Mary Henrietta, 1862-1900. 2. Explorers. 3.
Women—Biography. 4. Africa, West—Discovery and exploration. 5.
Congo River Valley—Discovery and exploration.] I. Title. II. Series.
  DT476.23.K56W34 2004
  916.604'312'092—dc22

                                                         2003026139

Table of Contents

Introduction

By Milbry Polk

Curiosity is one of the most compelling forces of human life. Our desire to understand who and what and where we are drives us restlessly to explore and to comprehend what we see. Every historical era is known by the individuals who sought to expand our boundaries of time and space and knowledge. People such as Alexander the Great, Ibn Battuta, Marco Polo, Ferdinand Magellan, Hernando de Soto, Meriwether Lewis, William Clark, Charles Darwin, Sir Richard Burton, Roald Amundsen, Jacques Cousteau, Edmund Hillary, Tenzing Norgay, Thor Hyerdahl, and Neil Armstrong are men whose discoveries changed our worldview. They were explorers, leaders into the unknown. This series is about a handful of individuals who have been left out of the history books but whose feats loom large, whose discoveries changed the way we look at the world. They are women explorers.

WHAT MAKES SOMEONE AN EXPLORER?

The desire to know what lies beyond the next hill—the desire to explore—is one of the most powerful of human impulses. This drive makes us unique among the species with which we share our earth. Curiosity helped to impel our remote ancestors out of Africa. It is what spread them in waves throughout the world where they settled; curiosity helped them adapt to the many environments they encountered.

Myths of all cultures include the memories of early explorations. These myths were the means by which people explained to themselves and taught their children about life, about the world around them, and about death. Myths helped people make sense of the inexplicable forces of nature and the strangeness of new lands and peoples. The few myths and legends that have come down to us are the stories of early exploration.

What makes someone an explorer? The qualities required are not unique. We are born explorers. Every child, even in the crib, is reaching out, trying to understand, to take the measure of its own body, then its immediate surroundings, and we continue as we go through life to grasp ever-widening circles of experience and reality. As we grow up, we often lose the excitement of the child, the characteristic that supposedly gave Albert Einstein his ability to see the universe in a new way. What typifies the explorer is not losing this wonderful childlike curiosity. He or she still reaches out. Explorers are open minded—able to look at and accept what they see, rather to fall back upon preconceived notions. Explorers are courageous, not just in facing physical danger, but also in having the courage to confront failure, ridicule, and laughter, and yet to keep on going. Above all, explorers have the ability to communicate. All insights, observations, and discoveries mean nothing to the wider community if they are not documented and shared. An explorer goes out into the world at some personal risk and discovers something of value and than shares that knowledge with his or her community. Explorers are leaders who look at the world in new ways and in doing so make breakthroughs that enrich all of our lives.

WOMEN EXPLORERS

Women, like men, have always been explorers. Typically in a "hunter-gatherer" society the men hunted animals while the women ventured far from the camps in search of other foods. Though their tasks were different, both were explorers. And, since such societies were almost constantly on the move, women were there for each voyage of discovery. But over time, as cultural groups became more settled, ideas began to change about the role of women in society. Women came to be restricted to the house, the shared courtyard, or the village and began to wear clothing that set them apart. By the time of the Middle Ages often the only way women in the Western world could travel was by going on pilgrimage. The trek to visit holy sites offered women one of the few opportunities to see new places, hear new languages, and meet different people. In fact, the first autobiography in the English language was written by a pilgrim, Margery Kempe (1373–1440), about her journeys throughout Europe and to the Holy Land.

Over time, women became formally excluded from exploration. Of course, some women did manage to find a way around the obstacles. Those who did venture forth went alone or in disguise and often needed men to help them. But their stories were not recorded in official histories; to find their stories one has to dig deep.

About three hundred years ago, the western worldview changed. Beginning in the 1700s, the scientific revolution began to change life for everyone in Europe. Men as well as women were swept up in the excitement to classify and understand every aspect of life on earth. Legions of people went to every corner of the world to see and record what was there. The spirit of adventure began to find new means of expression. New modes of transportation made movement around the world easier and new technologies made recording events and communication less expensive and more vivid.

The findings of these explorers were fascinating to the people back home. Wealthy individuals collected many of the strange insects, botanical specimens, native art, rocks, and other findings, brought back by the explorers into personal collections called Cabinets of Curiosities. These Cabinets of

Curiosities are the forerunners of our modern museums. The desire to collect the unusual financed expeditions, which in turn fostered public interest in exploration. The creation and spread of scientific and popular magazines with stories about expeditions and discoveries enabled the public to learn about the world. By the 1800s, explorers had the status of popular heroes in the public eye. The lure of the unknown gripped society.

Unlike men, women did not have support of institutions such as universities, museums, scientific societies, governments, and the military that sponsored and financed exploration. Until well into the twentieth century, many of these institutions barred women from participation, membership, and especially leadership. Women were thought capable of gathering things such as flowers or rocks for subjects to paint and draw, but men were the ones who studied them, named them, and published books about them. Most women, if they had any specialized education at all, gained it through private tutors. Men went to the university. Men formed and joined scientific societies and the exploring clubs. Men ran the governments, the military, and the press, and archived the collections. Universities and other cultural institutions were open only to the membership of men. Women were generally excluded from them. When these institutions sponsored exploration, they sponsored men. Women not only had to overcome mountains in the wild but also institutions at home.

In the 1800s women were not usually trained or taught academics. Instead, they learned sewing, music, and how to behave as a lady. A woman who managed to learn to write overcame great obstacles. Few managed to do it, but the same spirit that made women into explorers animated their minds in other ways. A few women learned to record what they were doing sufficiently well that at least some of their works have become classics of description and adventure.

Because of them, we know the little we do know about their lives and actions. As the nineteenth century progressed, more and more women were going out collecting, recording, and writing about faraway places. By the late 1800s more women were educated and those who traveled often wrote accounts of their journeys. So, now, in the twenty-first century, we are just beginning to learn about the unknown side of exploration—the women's story—from the accounts that lay buried in our archives.

And what a story it is. For example, one of the first modern women explorers was Maria Sybila Merian, who sailed to Surinam in 1699 at the age of 52. Not content to view the strange flora and fauna that were arriving back in Europe to fill the Cabinets of Curiosity, she wanted to collect and paint insects and animals in their native habitat.

Western women also faced societal obstacles; they generally could not go anywhere without a chaperon. So for a would-be woman explorer, a night in the wild spent in the company of a man who was not a close relative or her husband was unthinkable. And then there were the unsuitable clothes. In many parts of the early modern world it was punishable by death (as it was in Spain in the 1600s) or imprisonment (as it was in America well into the late 1800s) for women to appear in public wearing pants.

The heavy, layered dresses and tight corsets thought necessary for women made traveling very cumbersome. For example, when the Alps began to be climbed by explorers in the 1800s, a few women were caught up in the mania. The first two women to summit the Matterhorn climbed in skirts and corsets. The third woman, an American professor of Latin, Annie Smith Peck (1850–1935), realized the absurdity of leaping crevasses, climbing ice walls, and enduring the winds in a skirt. So, she wore pants. This created such a sensation in 1895 that the Singer Sewing

Machine Company photographed her and included a card with her in climbing gear with every machine it sold.

THE WOMEN EXPLORERS SERIES

When asked why he wanted to climb Mount Everest, George Mallory famously replied "Because it's there." Perhaps another explorer would answer the same question, "Because I don't know what is there and I want to find out."

Although we all have curiosity, what separates explorers is their willingness to take their curiosity further. Despite the odds, a lack of money, and every imaginable difficulty, they still find a way to go. They do so because they are passionate about life and their passion carries them over the barriers. As you will discover, the women profiled in this series shared that passion. Their passion gave them the strength to face what would seem to be insurmountable odds to most of us. To read their stories is more than learning about the adventure, it is a guide to discovering our own passions. The women in this series, Mary Kingsley, Gertrude Bell, Alexandra David-Néel, Annie Montague Alexander, Sue Hendrickson, and Sylvia Earle, all join the pantheon of explorers, the heroes of our age.

These six women have been chosen because their interests range from geographical to cultural exploration; from traversing the highest mountains to diving to the depths of the oceans; from learning about life far back in time to looking forward into the future. These women are extraordinary leaders and thinkers. They are all individuals who have braved the unknown and challenged the traditional women's roles. Their discoveries have had remarkable and profound effects on what we know about the world. To be an explorer one does not have to be wealthy or have multiple degrees. To be an explorer one must have the desire from within and focus on the destination: the unknown.

Mary Kingsley (1862–1900) was the daughter of an English Victorian gentleman-explorer who believed women did not need to be educated. Mary was kept at home and only tutored in German to translate articles her father wanted to read. But while he was away, she went into his library and educated herself by reading his books. She never married and followed the custom of her day for unmarried women by staying home with her parents. When her parents died she found herself alone—and suddenly free. She purchased a ticket to the Canary Islands with her inheritance. Once there, she learned about the Congo, then considered by the Europeans to be a terrifying place. When Kingsley decided to go to the Congo, she was warned that all she would find would be festering swamplands laced with deadly diseases and cannibals. Kingsley viewed that warning as a challenge. Having used up all her money on the ticket, she outfitted herself as a trader. She returned to the Congo, and in a wooden canoe she plied the tributaries of the Congo River, trading goods with the natives and collecting fish for the British Museum. She learned the languages of the interior and befriended the local tribes. She became an expert on their rich belief systems, which were completely unknown in Europe. Like many explorers, Mary Kingsley's knowledge bridged separate worlds, helping each understand and appreciate the other.

Gertrude Bell (1868–1926) was the daughter of a wealthy English industrialist. She had tremendous ambition, which she used to convince her parents to give her an education at a time when, for a woman, education was considered secondary to a good marriage. As a result of her intelligence and determination, she won one of the few coveted spots for women at Oxford University. After college, she did not know what to do. Girls of her class usually waited at home for a proposal of marriage. But after Bell returned home, she received an invitation from her uncle to visit Persia (modern-day Iran). Quickly, she set about learning Persian. Later she learned Arabic and begin her own archeological trips into the Syrian deserts.

When World War I broke out, Bell was in the Middle East. Her ability to speak the language, as well as her knowledge of the local tribes and the deserts from her archeological work, caused the British to appoint her to one of the most important jobs in the Desert War, that of Oriental Secretary. The Oriental Secretary was the officer of the embassy who was expected to know about and deal with local affairs, roughly what we call a political officer in an embassy. Bell played a major role in crafting the division of the Middle East into the countries we know today. She also founded the museum in Iraq.

Alexandra David-Néel (1868–1969) was performing in the Paris Opera when she married a banker. As she now had some financial freedom, she decided to act on her lifelong dream to travel to the East. Soon after she married, she sailed alone for India. She assured her husband she be gone only about 18 months; it would be 24 years before she would return home. Upon arriving in India she became intrigued with the Buddhist religion. She felt in order to understand Buddhism, she had first to master Tibetan, the language in which many of the texts were written. In the course of doing so, she plunged so deeply into the culture that she became a Buddhist nun. After several years of study, David-Néel became determined to visit the home of the spiritual leader of the Tibetan Buddhists, the Dalai Lama, who resided in the Holy City of Lhasa, in Tibet. This was quite a challenge because all foreigners were forbidden from entering Lhasa. At the age of 55, she began a long and arduous winter trek across the Himalayas toward Tibet. She succeeded in becoming the first Western woman to visit Lhasa. After returning to France, David-Néel dedicated the rest of her long life to helping Westerners understand the beauty and complexity of Buddhist religion and culture through her many writings.

A wealthy and restless young woman, Annie Montague Alexander (1867–1950) decided to pursue her interests in science and nature rather than live the life of a socialite in San Francisco. She organized numerous expeditions throughout the American West to collect flora, fauna, and fossils. Concerned by the rapid changes occurring due to the growing population, Alexander envisaged a time, all too soon, when much of the natural world of the West would be gone due to urbanization and agricultural development. As a tribute to the land she loved, she decided to create the best natural history museum of the American West. She actually created two museums at the University of California, Berkeley, in which to house the thousands of specimens she had assembled. In the course of her exploration, she discovered new species, seventeen of which are named for her. Though little known, Alexander contributed much to our knowledge of American zoology and paleontology.

Two women in this series are still actively exploring. Sue Hendrickson dropped out of high school and made a living by collecting fish off the Florida Keys to sell to aquariums. An invitation to go on an underwater dive trip changed her life. She became passionate about diving, and soon found herself working with archeologists on wrecks. Hendrickson was often the lead diver, diving first to find out what was there. She realized she had a knack for seeing things others missed. On land, she became an amber collector of pieces of fossilized resin that contained insects and later became a dinosaur hunter. While on a fossil expedition in the Badlands of the Dakotas, Hendrickson discovered the largest *Tyrannosaurus rex* ever found. It has been named Sue in her honor. Depending on the time of year, she can be found diving in the sunken ancient port of Alexandria, Egypt, mapping Spanish wrecks off Cuba's coastline, or in the high, dry lands of ancient forests hunting for dinosaur bones.

Sylvia Earle began her exploration of the sea in the early days of scuba. Smitten with the undersea world, she earned degrees in biology and oceanography. She wanted more than to just study the sea; she wanted to live in the sea. In the early 1970s, Earle was eager to take part in a project in which humans lived in a module underwater for extended periods of time for the U.S. Navy. Unfortunately, when the project was about to begin, she was informed that because she was a woman, she could not go. Undaunted, Earle designed the next phase of the project exclusively for women. This project had far-reaching results. It proved to the U.S. military that women could live well in a confined environment and opened the door for women's entry into the space program.

Earle, ever reaching for new challenges, began designing and testing submersibles, which would allow a human to experience the underwater world more intimately than anything created up to that time. Approaching age 70, her goal is to explore the deepest, darkest place on earth: the 35,800-foot-deep Marianas Trench south of Guam, in the Pacific Ocean.

The experiences of these six women illustrate different paths, different experiences, and different situations, but each led to a similar fulfillment in exploration. All are explorers; all have given us the gift of understanding some aspect of our world. All offer tremendous opportunities to us. Each of us can learn from them and follow in their paths. They are trailblazers; but many trails remain unexplored. There is so much unknown about the world, so much that needs to be understood. For example, less than 5 percent of the ocean has been explored. Thousands of species of plants and animals wait to be discovered. We have not reached every place on earth, and of what we have seen, we often understand very little. Today, we are embarked on the greatest age of exploration. And we go armed with more knowledge than any of the explorers who have gone before us.

What these women teach us is that we need explorers to help us understand what is miraculous in the world around us. The goal for each of us is to find his or her own path and begin the journey.

1

A New
Destination

It was August 1893 when a tall, fair-haired, 31-year-old Englishwoman decided to leave behind everything that was familiar. Her life, until that point, had been confined by the limited choices available to an unmarried woman in Victorian England and by the demands of a needy father and mother. However, both her parents had died little more than a year earlier, and their daughter, after having put aside her own dreams to care for her mother and father, felt a desperate need to leave her unhappy home behind.

Mary Kingsley would later describe this transforming journey as if it had happened by chance. "For the first time in my life," she wrote, "I found myself in possession of five or six months which were not heavily forestalled, and feeling like a boy with a new half-crown, I lay about in my mind . . . what to do with them."[1] The choice of a long journey was not made simply for lack of anything better to do, however, nor was her destination chosen merely at random. As a girl, Kingsley had relished the adventures of great African explorers like David Livingstone, Richard Burton, and John Speke, as well as the accounts of Paul Belloni Du Chaillu and Pierre Savorgnan de Brazza, who wrote of encounters with pygmies and gorillas while they explored remote regions of Western Africa.

Kingsley chose Africa for the adventure it promised, for the opportunity to witness a new world, unlike anything she had seen in her sheltered life as a woman whose adult years had largely been spent caring for her mother and, later, her father as well. After her parents' deaths, she spent several months sorting out the details of their funerals, and then settling their estates, as well as functioning as a housekeeper for her younger brother. It was only when these details had been taken care of, and when her brother announced his own intention to make a trip to the East, that Kingsley allowed herself to choose a new path. She felt depressed, even ready to die. She decided to go to Africa.

She shared her decision to travel to West Africa with friends, who cautioned her with tales of others who had gone to the African continent and never returned. She spoke with doctors, who told her of the many frightening diseases she could expect to encounter. Nevertheless, her research served only to confirm her desire to make the trip.

Kingsley was given specific advice about the sorts of things she would need, should she decide to make the journey to West Africa, and the result was a fairly cumbersome set of luggage for her first trip. She packed two diaries—one for scientific and geographical information, the other to serve as a personal journal. She brought clothing of the same type she wore in London and Cambridge—things like long black skirts, white blouses, and black leather boots—ignoring the dramatic differences in temperature between England and Africa. She carried photography equipment, including a tripod and heavy photographic plates, which were quite awkward in those early days of photographic art; collector's kits and specimen bottles of formaldehyde to gather exotic specimens of fish and insects for British museums; a bag containing basic medical supplies; and a long, waterproof sack that closed at the top with a bar, in which she hid blankets, boots, books, and a revolver and knife.[2]

A friend had provided Kingsley with a phrase book for her journey, but the book began with the translation for "Help, I am drowning," and continued with a series of rather alarming phrases, including the translations for "The boat is upset," "Get up, you lazy scamps," and "Why has not this man been buried?"[3] Kingsley decided to leave the phrase book behind.

The boat on which Kingsley made her first journey was a cargo ship rather than a passenger liner. Her fellow travelers were, for the most part, government officials and traders. When she boarded the boat at Liverpool, there were only two other women on board, and they both left the ship when it docked at the Canary Islands. Kingsley, despite being the only woman on board as the ship made its way south toward the West African coast, was treated well by her fellow passengers, who shared their experiences of their own previous journeys to West Africa, making frequent mention of various unusual diseases and the deaths of people they had known.

As the ship sailed on, many on board did become sick, but Kingsley remained healthy and was able to assist in nursing those fellow passengers who were ill. The ship encountered torrential downpours as it neared the African continent (Kingsley had unknowingly selected the wet season for her first journey, the worst time to sail to Africa). Violent tropical storms rocked the ship before it finally neared the coast of Sierra Leone and put down its anchor. Thick mist made it impossible for Kingsley to see her destination until the next day.

THE FIRST JOURNEY

Kingsley wrote that she felt frightened as the reality of what she was undertaking clearly presented itself to her in the bright light of a sunny morning. "On my first voyage out I did not know the Coast, and the Coast did not know me, and we mutually terrified each other," she explained in *Travels in West Africa*.[4] She was not reassured by the fact that the steamboat agents from whom she had purchased her ticket had calmly informed her that they made it a practice never to sell round-trip tickets for West African steamers, as frequently only a one-way ticket was required.

The harbor of the British colony of Sierra Leone was impressive when viewed from the ship. Kingsley could see low hills covered with tropical forests rising from the yellow, sandy shore, interrupted by creeks and bays. There were palm trees and cottonwoods, and large mountains, including one known as Sugar Loaf, covered with tropical plants.

Kingsley and the other passengers made for shore. Her first step on African soil was made at Freetown, the capital of Sierra Leone. The name came from the colony's role of providing a home for freed slaves, but the city was truly a melting pot of freed slaves from various parts of the world, as well as natives, British traders, and missionaries. From the harbor, Freetown seemed to consist of a series of impressive buildings made of gray stone, but Kingsley soon learned that the town's reputation of being lovely when viewed from the sea meant that it was much less lovely when viewed close up.

The stores and houses were dilapidated. Some were made of painted wood with iron roofs; others had thatched roofs covered with creeping plants and insects. The air was heavy and humid, and Kingsley could smell the distinctive perfume of frangipani, magnolia, oleander and rose, as well as other odors "that demonstrate that the inhabitants do not regard sanitary matters with the smallest degree of interest."[5]

A few stores and churches were made of a distinctive, local, red stone and covered with ferns and flowering plants displaying red or yellow flowers. The streets were unpaved, but covered with grass and earth trampled down by many, many feet.

Kingsley first arrived in Freetown on its busy market day, and the town was bustling. People hurried past, carrying on their heads packages, logs, planks of wood, blocks of building stone, containers of palm oil, or baskets of vegetables. There was great noise and confusion, as people bumped into each other, stopped suddenly for a chat, or paused to rearrange their bundles. Goats and sheep wandered freely through the streets, adding to the confusion. Huge, ugly turkey vultures sat on the top of a large cathedral.

When Kingsley was finally escorted to the home of a British trading agent, she found little relief from the heat or the animals. A dog-faced monkey startled her, an ostrich pecked one of her companions, and then, dramatically, a large brown cloud of locusts descended on the city.

Kingsley would soon become an expert on West African insects, later writing:

> [Seventy-five] percent of West African insects sting, 5 percent bite, and the rest are either permanently or temporarily parasitic on the human race. And undoubtedly one of the many worst things you can do in West Africa is to take any notice of an insect. If you see a thing that looks like a cross between a flying lobster and the figure of Abraxis on a Gnostic gem do not pay it the least attention, never mind where it is; just keep quiet and hope it will go away—for that's your best chance; you have none in a stand-up fight with a good thorough-going African insect.[6]

These first hours were a frightening introduction to the Africa of which Kingsley had dreamed. She did not turn back, but continued on, exploring the coastline, venturing to Cape Coast, Accra, the Bight of Benin, Bonny, and St. Paul de Loanda. She then headed inland and traveled north through Cabinda, the Congo Free State, French Congo, Cameroon, and Calabar. During the four months of traveling, she began to understand how little she really knew about Africa—and how much she wanted to learn more. "One by one I took my old ideas derived from books and thoughts based on imperfect knowledge and weighed them against the real life around me, and found them either worthless or wanting," she wrote.[7]

Kingsley witnessed scenes of spectacular beauty. She saw plants and animals so exotic and colorful it was difficult to believe they were real. She encountered people very different from those she had known in England and found that she was accepted by them in a way that she, an unmarried, middle-aged woman, had never felt accepted at home. Kingsley would spend the rest of her life visiting, writing about, and dreaming of Africa. The fear she first felt as the Sierra Leone coastline came into view faded and was replaced by an almost fearless appreciation of the world she was to explore. She drove away an attacking leopard by throwing a water jug at its head. She repelled a crocodile that tried to climb into her canoe by hitting it on the head with her paddle. She waded through leech-infested swamps and climbed 13,760-foot-high Mount Cameroon, becoming the first white woman to reach its peak. She ventured into jungles known to be inhabited by cannibals and traded with the tribes she encountered. As Mary Kingsley wrote in her book *Travels in West Africa*:

> As she studied new horizons, her own horizons and her beliefs about what her life could be changed dramatically. In seeking to visit a new world, she had found a new life. The west coast of Africa is like the Arctic regions in one particular . . . and that is that when you have once visited it you want to go back there again; and now I come to think of it, there is another particular in which it is like them, and that is that the chances you have of returning from it are small . . . [8]

2

Life Behind
the Shutters

In 1899, Mary Kingsley offered a poignant glimpse of her childhood. The famed explorer and adventurer had not spent her youth roaming the countryside searching for interesting bits of plant and animal life, as many expected. Instead, she had lived the earliest part of her life shut away from most of society, confined by the demands of a sick mother and an absent father. Kingsley later wrote of her childhood:

> The whole of my childhood and youth was spent at home, in the house and garden. The living, outside world I saw little of, and cared less for, for I felt myself out of place at the few parties I ever had the chance of going to, and I deservedly was unpopular with my own generation, for I knew nothing of play and such things. But this was not superiority of mind in me, at all; the truth was I had a great amusing world of my own other people did not know, or care about—that was in the books in my father's library.[9]

That Kingsley was able to read the books in her father's library, let alone go on to write her enduring accounts of her own travels, is astonishing proof of the fierce determination that disciplined her entire life. For she received no formal education, never went to school, and saw little of the world.

Mary Kingsley's relatives included intellectuals, writers, and explorers on her father's side. Her grandparents, Charles Kingsley Sr. and Mary Lucas Kingsley, had seven children, one of whom died as an infant, and one of whom it is believed committed suicide as a teenager. The four surviving sons— Charles Jr., Gerald, George, and Henry—all made their mark by writing or exploring, building a legacy that would continue in George's daughter, Mary.

First, there was Charles Kingsley Jr., who followed his father's example by pursuing a career in the church, becoming the curate of Eversley in Hampshire in 1842. Charles was no ordinary clergyman, however. He believed strongly that religion had a critical role to play in politics and was disturbed by the vast divisions in English society between the classes. Kingsley, and other supporters of the Christian Socialist movement, felt that the church had a responsibility to become involved in social problems, and his earliest writings, published under the pseudonym "Parson Lot," detailed his thoughts on the problems of the working class.

Charles Kingsley wrote at an astonishing pace, publishing numerous novels, including *Yeast*, which detailed the horrible conditions facing agricultural workers, and *Two Years Ago*, which detailed how poor public sanitation had contributed to a cholera outbreak. He published articles in numerous journals, some attacking the Catholic Church, others expressing his ongoing concerns with the terrible conditions under which workers in England operated. He wrote historical fiction, published collections of sermons, and even tackled the topics of marine biology and race and slavery in the United States.

As he grew older, Kingsley also began to write for children, first in *The Heroes or, Greek Fairy Tales for My Children*. Perhaps his most famous book, *The Water Babies*, was written for his youngest son and tells the story of a young chimney sweep who escapes from an unkind boss, falls into a river, and turns into a water baby who, traveling through the water, learns a variety of lessons from the marine creatures he meets.

Charles Kingsley became a professor of modern history at Cambridge and, in 1861, was appointed tutor to the Prince of Wales. Later in life, he explored the West Indies and spent six months traveling through the United States, both of which provided material for other books.

Charles' younger brother, Henry, also became a famous writer. Henry had traveled to Australia after failing to earn a degree at Oxford in 1853, hoping to make a fortune in the gold rush that was then underway. Henry did not strike it rich, however, and instead wandered from one menial job to another, occasionally even spending time begging for food and shelter. It was not a lifestyle that made a man wealthy, but it did provide him with a rich collection of experiences and stories. Henry's novelized account of his time in Australia was published in 1859 under the title *The Recollections of Geoffrey Hamlyn*, and earned him a certain amount of fame.

Henry wrote other novels, but none was ever quite as successful as his first. He married a woman who spent his money as fast as he could earn it, and in later years he frequently spent time at his brother George's house, escaping from an unhappy marriage by writing in his brother's attic or on the lawn. His tales of his adventures in Australia thrilled his young niece Mary, and although he died when she was still young, she would long remember his stories of how he had discovered an exotic, exciting world far from home.

Mary's uncle Gerald died before she was born, finding tragedy when seeking adventure like his brothers. In 1844, while serving as an officer in the Royal Navy, the 23-year-old Gerald and his shipmates on board the *Royalist* were stranded off the coast of Australia. Devastated by disease and unable to move in the becalmed sea, the crew first fell sick, and then began starving, and gradually dying. The commander was the first to die, followed by his officers, including Gerald, and then many crew members. His family learned of his death when his father overheard a conversation in which two gentlemen were discussing the fate of a ship in which the officers had all died, and those who had not died were eaten by cannibals. Then Charles Sr. realized, to his horror, that the ship being discussed was his son's ship, the *Royalist*.

IN SEARCH OF ADVENTURE

Although her Uncle Henry's tales of adventure in Australia and the reputations of her Uncle Charles and Uncle Gerald surely shaped Mary's imagination, it was her father who would ultimately have the greatest influence on the woman she became. In 1899, already a famous author because of her own two successful books on Africa, Mary would attempt to provide her father with a firm reputation of his own by gathering George Kingsley's papers and writings into a single memoir. George had co-authored one travel book, *South Sea Bubbles*, and left behind copious notes and ideas, but he had been absent for much of his daughter's youth, and the challenge of trying to create a memoir for man she little knew herself was daunting.

George Kingsley was born in 1826. Like his daughter, George found comfort in reading, and books of history and geography proved his favorites. He loved the tales of explorers, but the career he himself ultimately chose was much more practical: he decided to become a doctor. However, his love of adventure and curiosity about the world made him ill-suited to a settled career as a practicing family physician. Instead, he became the personal doctor for several wealthy men who loved to travel. He accompanied them on their journeys as their personal physician, and thereby was able to fulfill his own desire to explore the world. He worked first for the Marquis of Aylesbury, then later for the Dukes of Norfolk and Sutherland, and the first and second Earls of Ellesmere. These noblemen were, in general, quite healthy, so serving as their personal physician involved acting as their companion, traveling with them, and hunting and fishing with them, as much as providing any kind of medical care. He traveled first to the Mediterranean and then to Spain before gradually venturing farther and farther away from home, to Egypt, to Syria, to North Africa, and to the South Pacific.

Mary Kingsley admired the spirit of adventure that flourished in her father, but she paid a high price for the genes that would prompt her, too, to leave behind England in search of landscapes that were more exotic. For nearly 30 years, while George explored new settings, traveling in comfort with one or another wealthy patron, his family waited for him to come home.

AN UNFORTUNATE BEGINNING

Despite, or perhaps because of, George's unwillingness to settle down, his parents had held onto the hope that he might, at last, meet a suitable young woman and marry her. Since he was spending so much time in the company of wealthy young noblemen, it is understandable that his parents hoped he might meet a wealthy woman, perhaps an heir or daughter of a nobleman. The woman who George ultimately chose as his bride was far from suitable, and the circumstances of their marriage served to further isolate George from the rest of his family.

On October 9, 1862, in a small church in Islington, with only two witnesses, George Kingsley finally was married. The woman he had selected as his bride was 35-year-old Mary Bailey, an innkeeper's daughter who had worked for George as his cook. Four days after their wedding, she gave birth to their child, a daughter whom they named Mary Henrietta Kingsley.

It was not until after her parents' deaths that Mary learned of the circumstances of her parents' marriage and her own birth. While sorting through their papers she came upon her birth certificate and their marriage license and realized how, to give her legitimacy, her two mismatched parents had come together in what would prove to be an unhappy marriage. This fresh understanding certainly contributed to her own desire to flee her family home and all that was familiar, to leave England and all that it represented behind.

It is important to understand English society in the late 1800s to comprehend what Mary realized when she stumbled upon the reality of her parents' marriage and her own birth. The opportunities that existed for women in Mary Kingsley's day were quite limited and confined almost exclusively to marriage. It was viewed as extraordinary that she would venture forth, alone, into West Africa. Had her parents not married, had she remained the illegitimate daughter of a household servant, her future would have been even more limited. The best that she could have hoped for was to work, herself, as a servant.

By marrying Mary Bailey, George provided his daughter with legitimacy and Mary with a home in which to raise their daughter. However, for all practical purposes, that was all he provided. Barely three weeks after his wedding and the birth of his daughter, George Kingsley left home for a cruise on the Mediterranean. The ship periodically anchored at various comfortable ports, where George enjoyed picnic lunches on warm sandy beaches. In his journal, he noted how happy he was to be far away from "London the foggy with its dirty sloshing melting snow and cold rheumatising winds." [10]

While George enjoyed the perfumed air of Lisbon and other Mediterranean ports, Mary Bailey recovered from childbirth and her daughter began what would prove a lonely and isolated childhood. George's wife, although now given a certain amount of respectability by marriage, would never become respectable enough to be welcomed into his family. Even though George had elevated her when she became his wife, his family, and most of society, would continue to view her as what she had been: a servant hampered by her past and a heavy cockney accent.

Her marriage had also served to isolate her from her own family, who felt that she had risen above them. They never felt completely comfortable in her new world and certainly were uncomfortable around her husband. However, this was seldom a problem, as George was almost never at home.

For this reason, young Mary Kingsley grew up spending little time with either her father's or her mother's relatives. Social divisions meant that her mother was no longer suitable for the world from which she had come, nor respectable enough for the world into which she married. At first, the new mother became a kind of nurse for those who had no one to care for them, tending the sick and elderly. Gradually, Mary Bailey Kingsley herself became an invalid, seldom leaving her bed, suffering from a variety of vague symptoms that eventually required her daughter to care for her.

CHILDHOOD MEMORIES

Mary Kingsley's adventures apparently began when she was still an infant. Family legends told of two narrow escapes that marked her earliest days. First, she nearly drowned not once, but twice, the first time plunging into a deep area while still in her baby carriage before being rescued; the second time when both she and her nanny fell into a deep pool before a man jumped into the water and saved them.

When Mary was not quite two years old, her father, who was briefly back in England, decided to move the family to Highgate, a rural area outside of London. He bought a small house, surrounded by a black fence, next to a Baptist chapel. It was there that Mary's brother Charles was born in 1866. The house, although the nicest in the neighborhood, was a modest three-story home, with a narrow garden in the back. The first floor contained a small living room and a study for George when he was at home, as well as a kitchen and laundry area in the back; upstairs was the master bedroom and a nursery for the two children. On the third floor was the attic—two rooms used by Henry Kingsley when he arrived to work on his novels.

Mary's favorite room in the house was her father's study, containing his library of books as well as souvenirs from his travels. She spent hours exploring new worlds from the pages of the books George kept on shelves that stretched from the floor to the ceiling. He collected classic works of fiction, ancient and modern tales of explorations around the globe, even medical books from his time in medical school. The library also contained an exotic assortment of things that George collected from various parts of the world.

In that library, Mary escaped to a new world, a world where adventurous men (for they were nearly all men) carved out new paths in unknown territories. Within the pages of those books, Mary found brighter, sunnier climates and exotic landscapes that made her childhood more bearable.

The magic of the library stood in stark contrast to the dim and gloomy walls in which Mary was confined. Her mother felt that sunlight was somehow harmful, and soon after the family moved into the house ordered that all of the windows in the front of the house be boarded up. Only a single window, above the door, was left open. When George was away from home, his wife also shuttered the back windows of the house, facing the garden, so that the house was nearly always dark and musty.

It is not surprising that George's rare visits home were such an occasion. When he arrived, he literally brought sunshine and fresh air with him, as at last the back windows would be unsealed.

A LIMITED EDUCATION

While other young girls of Mary's age and (upper middle-class) status were taught to read, to do some basic math, to gain an understanding of geography, and to play the piano and draw, these tasks were normally carried out by a governess or by the young woman's mother. In the Kingsley household, no governess was hired, and Mary's mother probably did not have enough of an education herself to pass anything on to her daughter. One of the few things Mary did learn from her mother was to speak with a Cockney accent, dropping her "H's" when talking. The habit would stay with her throughout her life, and surprise audiences whenever she gave lectures. Her brother, Charles (or Charley, as Mary called him), was given an expensive education, but Mary was left to teach herself as best she could.

How, exactly, she learned to read is not clear. It is possible that her younger brother told her what he was learning in school; she may also have taken his books when he was finished with them and taught herself to read. Through reading she gained a vast understanding of the world around her. Despite the vast knowledge she accumulated from books—an understanding that would gradually expand to include physics, chemistry, engineering, and even Latin—she would throughout her life remain self-conscious about her lack of formal education and continually apologize for it.

When Charley was away at school, her father was away on his travels, and her mother was confined to her bed, Mary was left to amuse herself. This she did most often with books. She later recalled that the library provided her with a broad, if odd, array of knowledge on a wide range of subjects:

> They were mostly old books on the West Indies, and old medical books, and old travel books and what not; fiction was represented in it by the works of Smollett, and little else. No one would believe the number, or character, of the books I absorbed. My favourites among them were Burton's *Anatomy of Melancoly*, Johnson's *Robberies and Murders of the Most Notorious Pirates*, and *Bayle's Dictionary*. When my father was home from one of his long and many journeys, new books used to come into the house, and although I did not like them as the old, yet they had to be read too. But just as I was coming to the conclusion that new books were unworthy of my serious attention, one turned up that fascinated me wildly. It was *Solar Physics*, by Professor Norman Lockyer. That book opened a new world for me.[11]

While scientific texts fascinated young Mary, it was the accounts of explorers that would firmly shape her later years. In the late 1800s, the newspapers were full of accounts of European explorers revealing the mysteries of the African continent. The great adventures of Henry Morton Stanley, of Dr. David Livingstone, and of Verney Lovett Cameron opened up a new world to Mary. Richard Burton's search for the source of the Nile was another story that made a deep impression on Mary, and his account of his adventures on the French Congo,

Two Trips to the Gorilla Land, was perhaps the book that most influenced her. Some 20 years after reading of Burton's adventures among the Fang people, Mary herself would retrace his steps, visiting the Fang and traveling to many of the spots Burton had described in his book.

Mary was also influenced by the African explorations of David Livingstone, who died while searching for the source of the Congo. When Mary was 12 years old, the account of his death filled the newspapers, and Livingstone's books, which focused not merely on the geography of Africa but also on its people, impacted Mary's own focus on the people of Africa in her books.

Other explorers similarly influenced Mary. She would later

H. M. STANLEY

The adventures of Sir Henry Morton Stanley inspired Mary Kingsley and many others to follow in his footsteps into Africa. H. M. Stanley was born in Wales in 1841, and given the name John Rowlands. At the age of 18, he joined the crew of a ship as a cabin boy, traveling to New Orleans, where he was given a job working for an American merchant named Henry Morton Stanley. He soon took his employer's name.

Stanley served in the Confederate Army during the Civil War, was captured at the Battle of Shiloh, and was finally discharged because of poor health. He served as a correspondent for the *New York Herald,* traveling as a reporter to cover the British army's battles in Ethiopia. In 1869, he was given the assignment of traveling to Africa to look for the Scottish explorer David Livingstone, who had disappeared while searching for the source of the Nile.

Stanley reached the eastern coast of Africa in January 1871, and then set off into the interior, accompanied by about 2,000 men. He finally found Livingstone 11 months later, reportedly greeting the sick explorer with the words, point to Paul Belloni Du Chaillu and Pierre Savorgnan de Brazza as her particular heroes. Both explored similar regions in the Gabon, traveling through rain forests and areas inhabited by gorillas and pygmies as they moved along the Ogooué River. What impressed Mary most was the West African territory they explored—uncharted territory, full of danger that required quick thinking and fearlessness.

Mary was not unique in her fascination with the tales of exploration and adventures in far-away worlds. Newspapers, magazines, and books in the nineteenth century were full of these accounts. The stories frequently served to emphasize the prevailing idea in Victorian England that the British were superior to the rest of the world, and had a responsibility to

"Dr. Livingstone, I presume?" Stanley cared for Livingstone until he had recovered, and then the two men explored Lake Tanganyika.

Stanley returned to Europe in 1872. One year later, *The Herald* once more sent him to Africa, this time to the western coast to report on British military efforts in the region now known as Ghana. In 1874, Stanley explored the interior of Africa, traveling south and navigating the Lualaba and Congo rivers to Livingstone Falls (which Stanley named). He traveled on to the Atlantic Ocean, reaching it in August 1877. Nearly half of his expeditionary force had died during the course of the journey.

Stanley died in 1904 following a long illness. In his obituary, *The Guardian* noted, "His name is inseparably connected with the story of the rediscovery of a continent. . . . The historian of the future cannot write the history of Africa without also mentioning the name of Stanley." *

* Obituary of Sir H. M. Stanley, *The Guardian*, May 11, 1904, *http://www.guardiancentury.co.uk/1899-1909/Story/.*

bring their ideas, their culture, and their way of life to those less fortunate. Missionaries and explorers traveled into what was described as "darkest Africa," carrying with them a firm conviction that they could bring "light" (through religion, through trade, through their way of life) to these remote areas. David Livingstone wrote, "I view the end of the geographical feat as the beginning of the missionary enterprise," [12] outlining his idea that all of the different groups mapping out Africa—first explorers, then traders, scientists, missionaries, and political representatives—were all together working to improve the way of life for Africans. Mary Kingsley would take quite a different view, distinguishing between the efforts of scientists and traders, who she believed studied rather than changed African culture, and the actions of the missionaries and politicians, whom she generally deplored.

In the mid-1890s, in a lecture before a group of scholars and civil servants in England, Kingsley noted the irony of Europeans who went to Africa with the aim of "improving" the life of Africans. In Kingsley's view, African culture required little improvement:

> Had the African been that way disposed, there was nothing to have prevented his forming a great powerful culture state of his own before white aid or hindrance came. He flourishes in his climate; physically taken as a whole he is splendid; his country is fertile, rich in minerals from gold to coal, and well watered by a set of rivers which, also taken as a whole, you cannot surpass in the whole world. . . . after all, it all depends on what you regard as the criterion of perfection in a race, and I have had it pointed out to me that my criterion in this matter would barely do credit to a cave man of the Neolithic period; all I ask for in a race is courage, honour, a fine physical development, and an ability to make nature its slave instead of being hers. [13]

However, when Kingsley spoke these words she was very much in the minority. The British Empire was, at the time of Queen Victoria, the greatest in the world, and the explorers who braved the remote corners of Africa were proving it.

3

A Feeling of
Responsibility

As Mary Kingsley grew into a teenager, the shuttered existence at home must have felt stifling. With her mother confined to her bed with a variety of mysterious symptoms, it fell to Mary to manage the household, care for her mother, and help raise her brother. Her father would periodically reappear, linger for a month or two, and then set off on yet another journey.

Mary later admitted resenting her father's inability to understand how difficult his prolonged absences were on his family. While he was away, his letters home came irregularly if at all, and Mary's mother frequently imagined the worst, her anxiety adding to her illness. Although Mary certainly inherited her father's love of travel, his desire to explore new places, and his inability to feel settled and comfortable in England, still she combined it with a strong sense of responsibility and duty. Mary placed her sense of duty to her younger brother first; each time, before she set out for Africa, she first made sure that Charley was comfortable and had plans of his own. When he was at home, she felt that it was her responsibility to be there as well, to care for him and the house. This was, no doubt, a legacy of her childhood, a too-keen awareness of the cost of wandering the globe on those left behind. Kingsley wrote:

> I confess, that in the old days I used to contemplate with a feeling of irritation the way in which my father used to reconcile and explain it to himself, that because he had a wife and family it was his dire and awful duty to go and hunt grizzly bears in a red [sic] Indian-infested district, and the like. I fancy now that I was wrong to have felt any irritation with him. It is undoubtedly true that he could have made more money had he settled down to an English practice as a physician; also undoubtedly true that he thoroughly enjoyed grizzly bear hunting and 'loved the bright eyes of danger'; still there was in him enough of the natural man to give him the instinctive

feeling that the duty of a father was to go out hunting and fighting while his wife kept the home. But I am fully convinced that his taking this view of life really caused the illness, which killed my mother. For months at a time she was kept in an unbroken strain of anxiety about him.[14]

Kingsley spent her childhood and adolescence essentially isolated in her home, caring for her mother and brother. She had no girl friends, spent little if any time with her relatives, and because of her mother's illness, had no real role model from which to understand how young women behaved. Other upper middle-class Victorian teenaged girls would be attending parties and dances; Kingsley instead focused on learning as much as she could from books.

She studied science and engineering texts, sometimes with sadly comical results. Kingsley later remembered:

At this time I developed a passionate devotion for the science of chemistry and I went in for it—experiments not being allowed—in the available books in the library. Most of them were books on alchemy and the rest obsolete. After most carefully getting up all the information these could give me, I happened on a gentleman who knew modern chemistry and tried my information on him. He said he had not heard anything so ridiculous for years, and recommended I should be placed in a museum as a compendium for exploded chemical theories, which hurt my feelings very much and I cried bitterly at not being taught things.[15]

Following this embarrassing episode, Kingsley gradually realized that she could devise her own experiments to help her better understand science and engineering. She became expert at performing household repairs when the family moved to a new home in northwest Kent in 1879. The move had been made in the hope of improving Mrs. Kingsley's health; the Kent location was more rural and it was thought that the country air might be more healthful. The house needed frequent repairs: the doors and shutters needed to be replaced, the plumbing was unreliable—and so Kingsley taught herself through trial and error.

She was aided by one of the few neighbors the Kingsleys had in their more remote location, an electrical engineer named C. F. Varley. Varley was impressed by Kingsley's desire to learn, and he loaned her books and taught her engineering. Kingsley also was given her only formal education in Kent—her father wanted her to serve as his research assistant, and so he paid for a series of German lessons so that she could help research the German texts he needed for background information. She quickly absorbed the lessons and became fluent in German, but her father never remained in England long enough for their project to effectively begin. He was too busy exploring a new frontier—the American continent—traveling from Canada to Florida, then west to New Mexico and Wyoming. Then he traveled on to Japan, New Zealand, and Australia, finally returning when his son, Charley, was ready to attend a university. By this time, Mary Kingsley had grown up.

A NEW MOVE

By the time most young women reached their twenties in the late nineteenth century, they were expected to be married. In their late teens, they would have attended numerous parties, teas, and dances; been introduced to a wide range of suitable young men; and quickly paired off in marriage.

Mary Kingsley was an attractive young woman, tall and slim, with long, gold hair and a fashionably pale complexion. However, she had had no introduction to society, spent most of her time studying books, and was never in the company of young men. By the time she reached 20, she dressed in sober, black gowns and pulled her hair snugly back from her face in a tight bun. She was not yet an "old maid," but she was already dressing like one.

George Kingsley made a dramatic decision. He wanted Charley to attend Cambridge University, and decided to move his entire family to that town in 1884. Charley lived on campus, but the family settled in a new, three-story home only a few blocks from the university.

The move was accompanied by yet another dramatic change: George Kingsley, by now 60 years old, decided that the time had finally come for him to settle down. Living in the center of a cosmopolitan university town, with her father to accompany her on walks and outings, and meeting her brother's college friends, Mary discovered a new world. Her father had many friends among the scholars and scientists at Cambridge, several of whom were invited to the family home for dinners. Mrs. Kingsley was still largely confined to her bed, so it was Mary's job to host her father and brother's friends during these meals. She shopped every day at the market, took long walks through town, and went on boat rides with her brother and his friends on the Cam River.

Her mother needed constant care and depended on Mary to prepare her food and push her wheelchair on the rare occasions when she ventured outside. Despite her mother's demands, Mary was able to enjoy an expanding circle, new places to explore, and new people to meet. For the first time in her life, she began to have female friends, generally the daughters of friends of her father or neighbors.

Through the conversations at the dinner table, she gradually became involved in the real world. Politics was a frequent topic of conversation, and of particular interest to the globetrotting George Kingsley was a meeting taking place in Berlin from 1884 to 1885, a meeting that was transforming the future of Africa.

THE BERLIN CONFERENCE

From November 15, 1884, to February 26, 1885, 14 nations gathered in Berlin to decide how best to carve up the African continent. The attendees included most of the European nations (except Switzerland) and the United States, but five powers essentially ran the meeting and most heavily influenced its outcome: France, Germany, England, Portugal, and an entity labeled "the International Association of the Congo," which was essentially acting on behalf of the Belgian king, Leopold II. Within this group of powers, the three most significant—France, Germany, and England—had been engaged in a scramble to seize control of various parts of the African continent.

Much of the meeting focused on who would gain control of two critical regions: the Niger River and the Congo delta. Humanitarian concerns only occupied a small portion of the discussions. Debates about the possibility of eliminating the slave trade produced little concrete action. Instead, the agenda centered on securing free trade in the Congo and free navigation of the Congo and the Niger Rivers. In the end, the Berlin Conference settled disputes among the various European powers anxious to establish a presence in Africa by carving the western part of the continent into pieces.

These divisions were made not because of extensive travel throughout Africa, but by diplomats in Germany, studying maps and looking for the best route for their goods. How these boundaries, arbitrarily drawn, would impact the tribes who might find themselves thus cut off from their hunting grounds or rivers was given little thought. These peoples were viewed, in general, as a kind of group—"African natives"—who would inevitably benefit from any exposure to European culture and civilization.

These boundaries would reap a lasting legacy of unrest and war. All of this was in the future, however. The Berlin Conference was held to finally settle who would occupy which part of West Africa. When its conclusions were announced, the attendees loftily declared that it was in the best interest of Africa and the entire world that all traders, missionaries, and representatives from all countries have free access to Africa's interior, to freely navigate the Niger and Congo Rivers, to bring European "civilization" to Africans.

The reality was quite different. Few steps would be taken to ensure that all countries had free access. Instead, most European powers were concerned about protecting their own rights, not those of other nations. As Mary Kingsley would find, the conference was particularly significant for its stipulation that no new European annexations along the African coastline would be officially recognized unless they were marked by "effective occupation;" in other words, unless the European power sent its own officials and soldiers to effectively maintain control over that territory.[16] In order to ensure that their territory was marked by "effective occupation," British officials joined the British traders and missionaries in policing their portion of the West African coast.

The newspapers carried detailed reports about the conference, focusing in particular on the way political divisions were personified by the explorers Kingsley and so many others admired: Pierre Savorgnan de Brazza, whose travels through the Congo had benefited France, and Henry Morton Stanley, who was acting on behalf of the Belgian king.

Although in the newspapers she was reading about borders being drawn in a distant part of the globe, Kingsley's own borders were much narrower—and nearly impossible to cross. The move to Cambridge had helped to expand her own circle, but Kingsley remained close to home. She finally made her first trip away from home when she was 25, a vacation with a friend and her family to Wales. After only two days, however, Kingsley was forced to return home. Her mother had become very ill as soon as Kingsley had left, and a telegram requested that Kingsley return home at once, which she did.

It would be nearly three years before Kingsley would attempt to leave home again, this time traveling with a friend to Paris. She spent one week there, but upon her return her mother became so ill that she demanded Kingsley's constant care. It soon became impossible for Kingsley to leave the house for more than an hour or two at a time, nearly completely restricting her social life.[17]

Soon her mother's care grew much more demanding. In 1890, she suffered a stroke, leaving her partially paralyzed and unable to feed or bathe herself, or even to speak in a way comprehensible to anyone but Kingsley.

Mary Kingsley was in her late 20s, and her own brief feelings of freedom had been snuffed out. She spent her days caring for her mother and her nights concentrating on her studies. She learned Arabic, Syrian, and Latin; studied anthropology and the physical sciences; and calmed her mother whenever she woke during the night. Later she would remember this part of her life as "years of work and watching and anxiety, a narrower life in home interests than ever, and a more hopelessly depressing one, for it was a long losing fight with death all the time."[18]

Soon she was nursing both parents. George Kingsley became ill with rheumatic fever. He recovered gradually, and feeling weaker, decided that the only thing that would cure him was a long journey. The trip weakened him even further, and on February 4, 1892, he died in his sleep. His wife would survive him by a little more than two months. On April 25, 1892, Mary Bailey Kingsley also died, leaving her 29-year-old daughter at a crossroads. She had spent nearly three decades of her life lonely and confined to a limited world. Now the prospect of a very different future faced her, one in which she could shape her own horizons and discover how much courage she possessed.

Duty still weighed her down, though, and Kingsley felt responsible first for sorting through her parents' papers and settling their estates, then caring for her brother Charles. She traveled to the Canary Islands only when Charles decided to leave for the Far East. It was while traveling that Kingsley first encountered traders from the western coast of Africa. Their stories, often grim, managed to inspire in Kingsley a desire to see the place personally.

She returned to England, moving to London and organizing the apartment she shared with her brother. When Charles once again set out, Kingsley felt free, and this time her destination was Africa. There she would discover a new world, a landscape that brought to her, for the first time, a feeling that she was at home.

4

Destination: Africa

Mary Kingsley's choice of West Africa as her destination was not whim or sudden impulse, although she breezily dismissed her journey in *Travels in West Africa* as the result of time on her hands that needed to be filled, and her destination as one chosen by process of elimination:

> Where on earth am I to go? I wondered, for tropics are tropics wherever found, so I got down an atlas and saw that either South America or West Africa must be my destination, for the Malayan region was too far off and too expensive. Then I got Wallace's Geographical Distribution and after reading that master's article on the Ethiopian region I hardened my heart and closed with West Africa. I did this more readily because while I knew nothing of the practical condition of it, I knew a good deal both by tradition and report of South East America, and remembered that Yellow Jack was endemic, and that a certain naturalist, my superior physically and mentally, had come very near getting starved to death in the depressing society of an expedition slowly perishing of want and miscellaneous fevers up the Panama.[19]

This rather breezy description gives the false impression that Kingsley simply decided to travel somewhere warm, picked up the atlas, and made her choice from ignorance of West Africa's real dangers. Kingsley was certainly much better informed than many others who traveled there. She had spent much of her childhood poring over the accounts of the explorers who had ventured into the Congo. On her recent journey to the Canary Islands, she had listened to the grim tales of the West African traders, and her father's accounts of his travels certainly informed Kingsley about the risks of such a journey.

Africa represented a kind of escape for Kingsley—an escape from the familiar, an escape from what had become a sad and limited life, an escape from her grief over the deaths of her parents, and an escape from the confines Victorian society placed upon a woman in her thirties. In traveling to a place so dramatically different from the world she had known, Kingsley would discover in herself new traits, such as courage, fearlessness, and boldness.

Victorian women did travel, but they generally did so on a large scale, accompanied by a maid and several trunks of clothing. A popular book for women travelers during Kingsley's day, *Hints to Lady Travelers at Home and Abroad* by Lilias Campbell Davidson, offered the following advice to women who might find themselves in trouble when traveling:

> As a broad general principle, a woman's place in the moment of danger is to keep still and be ready for action. It is so much an instinct with the stronger sex to protect and look after the weaker, that in all cases of the sort, if there is a man at the head of affairs, he had better be left to manage matters without the hampering interference of feminine physical weakness. If there is no man, the woman will have to act for herself, but even then she will find it the best plan to keep still till the decisive moment arrives.[20]

The choice of Africa as a destination posed a special challenge to Kingsley. The few women who traveled to Africa went with their husbands, most often as missionaries. In fact, it was not until the 1880s that single women were allowed to serve as missionaries in Africa. Those who did go generally went prepared to serve in multiple capacities—as missionaries, as nurses, and as teachers.

It was a difficult life, particularly for those women who went not because of a deep, personal desire to see the continent, but instead to accompany their husbands. The wife of explorer David Livingstone traveled with him to central Africa and died there in 1862. Anna Martin Hinderer traveled with her missionary husband to Nigeria in 1853 and wrote frequent letters home to England outlining the difficulties and dangers of life in Africa. On January 1, 1862, she noted:

> War, so-called war, is still going on, with very little of real war, but roads shut up, and parties out kidnapping. We, of the mission in Ibadan, are the chief and almost the only sufferers; depending on the coast as we do, and with no road: European necessaries and comforts we have long been without and cannot have again. My last pair of shoes are on my feet, and my clothes are so worn and so few, that if the war does not end soon, I shall have to come to a country cloth, and roll up like a native. These would be small troubles if we were in health, but my dear husband is a sad sufferer, and every bit of remedy or alleviation, in the way of medicine, have been for some months entirely finished. I have had two most severe attacks of fever, one in August, and one in November. I only began to get out on Christmas Day, to the great pleasure of our people, who said it would be no Christmas at all if I were not with them. And I have been getting better ever since, creeping up hill, and falling by degrees into all my various duties; but recovering is slow work, when even a cup of tea can now only be taken sparingly, by way of a luxury, as very little is left. Goat meat and yams, though good enough at other times, are not very nourishing or congenial now, and the season is fearfully hot.[21]

Despite, or perhaps because of, the dangers Africa presented, Kingsley pressed ahead. West Africa had fascinated her for years. She was determined to see it for herself.

A BRIEF HISTORY
Despite the intense focus on West Africa as a valuable resource during the Berlin Conference, trade with Europe was certainly not

new. In the 1400s, European sailors, most often from Portugal, had navigated down the West African coastline, exploring it as far as the mouth of the Congo and eventually setting up trading stations. The focus for these explorers and their governments was much more on trade than on setting up government outposts or occupying territory. That would come later.

Trade blossomed first in such products as gold and pepper. Soon, slaves were added to the exports leaving Africa, as millions of West Africans were seized, thrown onto slave ships, and transported across the Atlantic. Their destination was the European colonies in America, where they served as cheap labor for the settlers.

The slave trade has been described as the most important single external influence on the life of West Africa for the three and a half centuries during which it flourished.[22] The numbers of West Africans seized and forced into slavery grew steadily, from 1530, when the slave trade with America essentially began, to the eighteenth century, when it was at its height. Approximately 2,200 Africans were enslaved per year in the sixteenth century; the number increased to 15,600 per year in the seventeenth century, to a horrifying 68,000 per year in the eighteenth century; it is believed that more than eleven million Africans were enslaved before the practice gradually died out in the late nineteenth century.[23] Many of them would not survive the brutal conditions of the trip across the Atlantic.

Portugal was not the only European power to recognize the opportunity trade with West Africa offered, including the trade in slaves. Dutch traders soon established their own outposts along the West African coast, and as the demand for slaves to supply colonies in America and the West Indies increased, so too did the economic incentives for other nations to enter the slave trade. This trade in human beings is difficult for modern readers to comprehend, but it is important to understand how the relationship between West Africa and Europe evolved and how critical the slave trade was to that evolution.

Slave traders from Portugal were soon joined by those from England, France, and the Netherlands, as well as those from Sweden and Denmark.

These countries soon determined to form trading companies to better protect their interests in West Africa. Eventually, these trading companies built forts along the West African coast, where slaves and trade goods were brought from the interior of Africa and held until they were shipped elsewhere. The forts were necessary to ward off attacks by other nations or trading companies trying to increase their own influence or presence along the coast.

The competition among the nations and the frequent attacks against one fort or another soon left only a few nations holding the prize: control of the West African coast. By the 1700s, the French were firmly in control of the territory then known as Upper Guinea (the coastal region north of Sierra Leone), while the British and Dutch competed for control of the Gold Coast (where modern Ghana is found). Britain proved the ultimate victor, and soon France and Britain were facing each other on opposite sides for seven major wars. From the late 1600s to 1815, Britain and France fought for the dominant position in world trade. At the end of those wars, Britain found itself firmly in control of a significant portion of trade with West Africa.

OUTPOSTS ON THE RIVER

The presence of European trading posts along the West African coast dramatically altered the development of life there. As more and more trade and commerce revolved around the trading posts, their locations became the centers of power in the region. Towns grew up around the trading posts, populated by those who were increasingly dependent on the traders for their livelihood. Violence was an unpleasant fact in these towns, as rival merchants or Africans, or both, attacked a trading post to seize its goods or take over its position on the coast.

By the late eighteenth century, an anti-slavery movement was spreading in Europe. The movement was particularly strong in England and it finally resulted in the enactment of parliamentary law: the 1772 act that outlawed slavery in England, the 1807 act of Parliament that made it illegal for British subjects to engage in the slave trade in Africa, and the 1833 act that outlawed slavery throughout the British empire.

These laws were actively policed by the British navy, which seized ships carrying slaves and brought them to the territory of Sierra Leone. Sierra Leone soon became the destination for former slaves who had been set free, either by law in England or in America because of their service during the Revolutionary War, in which those who fought for England were promised freedom.

Ultimately, a group of abolitionists decided to formalize a settlement in Africa to serve as a destination for these former slaves. A company was created to trade with the interior of West Africa and, from the profits, pay for the administration of the new colony. In 1791, an act of Parliament formalized the creation of the Sierra Leone Company, and soon a settlement named Freetown, with European administrators and settlers who were former slaves, was established.

Gradually, the British government recognized the strategic significance of Sierra Leone as a valuable naval base along the African coast, and it took over the administration of Sierra Leone, making it a British colony. As more and more slave ships were seized, the freed slaves were brought to Freetown, and the colony grew rapidly.

Later in the nineteenth century, another colony of former slaves was created. These slaves had been set free in America, and the American Colonization Society, an organization founded in 1816 to find a new home for freed slaves, decided that the most appropriate resettlement would be in West Africa. The Society eventually obtained a grant to land near the Gabon River, at Cape Mesurado. Gradually, this territory would grow into the town of Monrovia, the capital of Liberia. Because the

United States was unwilling to establish a formal protectorate in Liberia, the settlement evolved into an independent republic, formally declared in 1847 and soon afterwards recognized by a number of European nations. The United States, however, did not formally recognize Liberia until 1862, when the divisive issue of slavery had exploded into civil war.

Although the intentions of the British and American abolitionists who created these colonies were generally good, it is important to understand that the result was the transport and settlement of thousands of Africans into areas having their own native populations. Thousands of former American slaves were brought to Liberia, and freed European slaves were brought to Sierra Leone, given some land and a certain amount of administrative power; the liberators did this while ignoring the rights of native Africans who already populated the region. It reflected a basic, mistaken view that "Africans were Africans"; tribal divisions and conflicts were ignored. The new settlers often did not get along with the natives, yet the majority of the power for the territory was theirs. The stage was being set for conflicts that would long outlive the Sierra Leone Company and the American Colonization Society.

IN SEARCH OF A RIVER ROUTE

To help facilitate the further development of trade in West Africa, trading companies began to turn their attention to developing better routes to transport goods from West Africa's interior to the trading posts along the coast. Soon these trading companies began financing expeditions to find the source of the great African rivers: the Congo and the Niger.

Several expeditions were financed to attempt to map the course of these rivers, find their sources, and determine whether or not trading opportunities existed with the tribes who lived along them. Mungo Park, Hugh Clapperton, and Richard Lander all led expeditions that provided valuable data about the course of the Niger River and, in turn, the geography of West Africa. Later explorers added to this knowledge, many of them focusing less on trade than on political opportunities for the countries funding their expeditions.

As the geography of the interior of West Africa became clearer, missionaries joined the traders in setting up camps. The earliest were Roman Catholics, and Protestants soon followed. The missionaries were supported by governments eager to extend their influence in West Africa. When France began to expand its presence in West Africa in the mid- to late nineteenth century, a large number of Catholic missions grew up there. Similarly, British missionaries traveled to Sierra Leone, the Gold Coast, and Nigeria, while American missionaries set up missions in Liberia.

The advent of missionaries in West Africa marked an important shift. Previous settlements, trading posts, and new colonies that provided homes for freed slaves had been created to the benefit of the host countries. Missionaries traveled to West Africa with a very different goal: to help the Africans. Mary Kingsley was frequently critical of the missionaries' techniques, particularly the education they attempted to impart on the tribes they encountered, for its focus on European customs and training, rather than valuable medical or agricultural techniques. "The mission does not undertake technical instruction," she observed of one French mission in *Travels in West Africa*:

> All the training the boys get is religious and scholastic. The girls fare somewhat better, for they get in addition instruction from the mission ladies in sewing, washing and ironing . . . the washing and ironing are quite parlour accomplishments when your husband does not wear a shirt, and household linen is non-existent.[24]

One result of the increasing influence of European missions and colonies was a diminishing recognition of the value and rightful place of African culture. As European control grew over West Africa, Europeans became less tolerant of African ways and beliefs and less willing to recognize the abilities of Africans themselves.[25] It became a popular belief among many Europeans that Africa needed European influence in order to become "civilized."

A CONTINENT OF COLONIES

By the time that Mary Kingsley prepared for her voyage to West Africa, much of the continent was officially under European control. With the exception of Liberia, all of West Africa had been partitioned and was designated as under the governance of one or another European nation. France controlled the largest portion; the second largest belonged to Britain; a total of four colonies separated by portions of French territory. Germany governed the colony of Togo and Cameroon. Portugal, once the dominant European power in West Africa, now governed the considerably smaller territory of Portuguese Guinea.

Although official maps of the late nineteenth and early twentieth century seemed to show a series of clear borders and boundaries marking off European colonies, the reality was quite different. Much of the land marked off as French or British territory was inhabited by tribes who had never seen a white face, who had no knowledge that they belonged to a European colony, and who would have refused to recognize its authority if they did.

The Berlin Conference had provided the European powers in West Africa with two mandates to justify expanding presence there: to stop the slave trade and replace it with European civilization, and to facilitate trade with Africa. Both of these mandates required increasing governmental and military presence in order to enforce them.

Mary Kingsley would discover the clear difficulties with the colonial policies of Britain, France, and the other European powers attempting to govern West Africa. The existence of kingdoms or tribes was often ignored. The people were grouped together as "Africans" or "natives" who needed to be ruled with a kind of "one policy fits all" attitude. While European powers often spoke in lofty terms of the need to bring "civilization" to Africa, as if its people were somehow inferior to Europeans, the real goal of the colonial states was to promote European interests.[26]

Mary Kingsley understood the danger in attempting to govern a people without any real understanding of their customs or climate, without any knowledge of their history or beliefs, and without any recognition of their value. In traveling to West Africa and writing of her experiences, she brought a new perspective. She traveled not as a tourist, but as a trader. She was able to view with an occasionally satirical eye the absurdity of the European influence in West Africa, and to understand how rapidly it was destroying much of value. "Now European governments are undertaking to legislate domestically for the African from European offices," Kingsley noted in a lecture in 1895 to an audience of scholars and civil servants:

> They cannot do this thing successfully unless they have in their possession a full knowledge of the nature of the people they are legislating for; without this, let their intentions be of the best, they will waste a grievous mass of blood and money, and fail in the end.[27]

5

At Home in a Foreign Land

The beginning of this book detailed Mary Kingsley's first voyage to Africa, and how it transformed her life. Nothing would ever be the same for her after that first trip, and the rest of her life was spent waiting until she could once more return to Africa.

When she returned after that journey, in January 1894, she found England cold and barren. There had been little to hold her to England before she left for Africa—only a sense of duty to her brother—but once she had seen the vivid colors and smells, experienced the thrill of dangerous travel, and met a new group of adventurous people, she viewed her time in England as a kind of exile.

She spent eleven months in England, caring for her brother while dreaming of Africa. She kept her memories alive by trying to recreate Africa in the London apartment she occupied with Charley. She had brought back a variety of souvenirs and mementos from her travels, and these were on display throughout the apartment—things like African masks and woven cloths, iron and bronze armlets, charms, and even a three-foot-high carved statue, which Kingsley named Muvungu, who was pierced with rusty nails and covered in dried blood.[28] Visitors to Kingsley's apartment would be greeted by the alarming sight of Muvungu waiting at the top of the stairs and overwhelmed by the tropical temperatures at which she kept the house heated.[29]

Kingsley also preserved her memories of Africa by writing them down. She used her diaries and letters to recreate her journey in a manuscript she titled *The Bights of Benin*. She wrote for several months before approaching Macmillan, the publishing company that had published her father's writing, to see if they would be interested in her manuscript. Kingsley needed money to help finance her travels, and her brother seemed unlikely to be able to support both of them. Macmillan offered her a contract, and even went so far as to set some of the manuscript pages, but the manuscript was never completed and published. While she wrote, Kingsley continued to read

voraciously, studying other anthropological texts and gradually realizing that her own research was not nearly detailed
enough or serious enough to merit publication.

Her focus shifted as her studying continued. Kingsley
realized that what she wanted to produce was not a series of
light-hearted observations of West Africa, but instead something more serious, something that would provide cultural and
scientific value to researchers. She set the manuscript aside;
later bits of it would be used in *Travels in West Africa*, in *West
African Studies*, and in her lectures.

Kingsley sorted through her father's writings, selecting
and editing material extracted from his journals and letters to
produce a work that would eventually be published as *Notes
on Sport and Travel*. She also proceeded with plans for her
return trip to West Africa.

Determined to provide research of lasting value, Kingsley
focused on what she labeled "fish and fetish." By *fetish*, she meant
the beliefs of the tribes she encountered, and indeed several
chapters of *Travels in West Africa* were devoted to her observations of the religious beliefs, customs and superstitions of the
tribes she observed. She also was determined to collect unusual
species of fish, which she planned to bring back for British
museums. Her mentor in this area was the keeper of the zoolog-
ical department of the British Museum, Albert Charles Günther.

Kingsley had brought back several specimens of fish from
her first trip to West Africa and shown them to Günther when
they first met. Günther had then instructed her in how better
to preserve her specimens, provided her with the necessary
equipment for collecting specimens, and told her which fish to
collect when she next traveled to West Africa. Specifically,
Günther told Kingsley that she should focus on collecting fish
from the region between the Congo and Niger rivers, a region
about which little was known. Günther explained to Kingsley
that specimens of fish from this little-explored region would
be particularly valuable, and this no doubt contributed to

Kingsley's decision to travel along the Ogooué River in the French Congo, the river that runs between the Niger and Congo rivers.

PLANS FOR DEPARTURE

While in England, Kingsley also met two men who were heavily involved in the administration of West Africa. One of these was Sir George Goldie, who was the head of the Royal Niger Company, one of the trading companies chartered by Britain following the Berlin Conference to protect British interests in West Africa. The Royal Niger Company helped ensure British control of the Niger River, but Kingsley admired Sir Goldie for his respect for the culture of West Africans, his recognition of their social and political structures. His company would demonstrate this philosophy.

Kingsley also was friendly with Sir Claude MacDonald, the royal governor of the Niger Coast Protectorate. This territory was east of the land controlled by Sir Goldie's Royal Niger Company, and at one point MacDonald was sent to inspect the territory and report on his successes and failures, ensuring that Sir Goldie and MacDonald would not become friendly. Indeed, each demonstrated the different approaches to British control of portions of West Africa. Under Sir Goldie, the Royal Niger Company held a trade monopoly, and demonstrated the British practice of *indirect rule* (in this case, indirectly governing a territory through a royally chartered company). In the Niger Coast protectorate, MacDonald governed his territory directly, using free trade, as a crown colony. The two men did have a common respect for the wishes and ideas of the Africans living within the territory they administered.

Kingsley was also friendly with MacDonald's wife, who had decided to join her husband in West Africa. Lady MacDonald, learning that Kingsley planned to return to West Africa, asked her to postpone her departure so they could travel together. Kingsley agreed, knowing that she would be better able to leave once her brother, had embarked on a journey he had planned to Singapore. She planned a much longer stay this time; knowing that her publisher was anxious to publish whatever she would write gave her a certain amount of freedom from financial worries.

Finally, as the end of 1894 approached, Charley set out for Singapore and Lady MacDonald announced that she was ready. On December 23, 1894, Mary Kingsley once more set sail for Africa.

ABOARD THE *BATANGA*

Thanks to the advice and assistance of Albert Charles Günther, Mary Kingsley was much better equipped for collecting specimens of fish when she again set out for the African coast. She carried with her numerous bottles and 15 gallons of "spirit." By the time she returned to England, she would bring back 65 species of fish, including 3 new species of fish that would be named for her, and 18 species of reptile.[30]

All of this was in the future. Kingsley offers a humorous description of Lady MacDonald's rather desperate efforts to be helpful to Kingsley's fish-collecting efforts immediately after they set sail. The women were traveling on the *Batanga*, a boat captained by Captain John Murray, whom Kingsley had met on her first trip to West Africa. Almost immediately after their departure from Liverpool, Kingsley noted, Lady MacDonald demonstrated her eagerness to assist Kingsley:

> During the earlier days of our voyage she would attract my attention to all sorts of marine objects overboard, so as to amuse me. I used to look at them, and think it would be the death of me if I had to work like this, explaining meanwhile aloud that "they were very interesting, but Haeckel had done them, and I was out after fresh-water fishes from a river north of the Congo this time," fearing all the while that she felt me unenthusiastic for not flying

over into the ocean to secure the specimens. However, my scientific qualities, whatever they may amount to, did not blind this lady long to the fact of my being after all a very ordinary individual, and she told me so—not in these crude words, indeed, but nicely and kindly.[31]

Once Lady MacDonald understood that Kingsley would not begin collecting specimens until reaching West Africa, the two women enjoyed each other's company. Kingsley did observe on board the *Batanga*, but these observations were not about fish. Instead, she made notes on the crew, which she would later publish in *West African Studies*, creating a kind of anthropological study of the sailors, referring to the officers as *nauta pelagius vel officialis* and noting that the position they occupy on the evolutionary scale "is easily determined by the band of galoon [*sic*] round his coat cuff; in the English form the number of gold stripes increasing in direct ratio with rank."[32]

The *Batanga* briefly stopped at the Canary Islands, and then traveled south, reaching Sierra Leone on the morning of January 7, 1895. Kingsley and Lady MacDonald traveled on to Cape Coast, staying there as the guests of Wesleyan missionaries Dennis Kemp and his wife, whom they had met on board their ship. The women were given a tour of the grand facades of Cape Coast Castle and Fort William.

From Fort William, Kingsley gazed out over the town below, getting a clear view of the solid stone buildings sprinkled among the mud huts, and the sparkling blue water of the sea. The heat was intense, and the women soon descended to a series of cool, clean tunnels, sealed by heavy, massive doors under the fort, which had been built to house slaves awaiting departure on slave ships. They then returned to the Wesleyan mission to spend the night.

Kingsley, despite her frequent criticism of missionaries and their efforts in West Africa, appreciated what Dennis Kemp and his wife were attempting at the Wesleyan mission on the Gold Coast. They had recently added a technical focus to the mission's education and religious curriculum, and Kingsley understood the value this would provide.

EARLY DAYS

Kingsley had plotted a course that would take her first along some of the port cities of the West African coast—from Sierra Leone to the Gold Coast, on to the Spanish island of Fernando Po, and then to Calabar. The focus of her journey would then lead her into the little known Gabon territory of the French Congo, before ending in Cameroon. She planned to spend the time in the Gabon territory, along the Ogooué River, gathering the valuable fish specimens that she had been told would greatly enrich current scientific knowledge. Gabon then lay within the part of West Africa known as French Congo. While the territory was held by France, American missionaries had established a mission and school in Glass, near Libreville, and both Protestant and Catholic missions lay along the river. There were also British traders along the river, whose trading houses maintained firm economic control over the territory. All of these groups, missionaries, French civil servants, and British traders, would aid Kingsley during her journey.

First, while still traveling with Lady MacDonald, Kingsley skirted the coast heading on to Accra, in what is now Ghana. Kingsley found Accra lovely when viewed from her boat, but less attractive when seen up close. The exotic outlines of Fort St. James and Christiansborg Castle provided a magnificent view when seen from a distance, but up close, Kingsley was less than impressed by the remaining buildings that made up the town, chiefly "a mass of rubbishy mud and palm-leaf huts, and corrugated iron dwellings for the Europeans."[33] She particularly disliked the corrugated iron structures, finding them unbearably hot during the day, and chilly and damp in the evenings.

Because she was traveling with Lady MacDonald, Kingsley enjoyed being hosted by the governor of Accra and meeting a king—an African king who had been granted a very limited rule over his people, that principally consisted of being held responsible for any wrongdoing his people might commit but unable to punish them in any serious way. She enjoyed a formal tour of Christiansborg Castle, noting that spray from the sea had left nearly everything in the castle covered with mold.

Finally, Kingsley accompanied Lady MacDonald to Calabar, where they were greeted by the entire community and an impressive display of fireworks. The MacDonalds traveled with Kingsley on to Spanish-held Fernando Po, still on board the *Batanga*. Kingsley had visited Fernando Po on her previous journey, but the presence of the MacDonalds opened additional doors and she was able to meet the governor of that territory. He was a former Spanish naval officer, had lived for a while in Cuba, and spoke English with an American accent. He told of his arrival at Fernando Po and his discovery that the previous governor had died of fever. Immediately after he learned this news, he too was stricken by fever and placed in the very bed where his predecessor had died only a short while before.

Upon his recovery, the governor swiftly built himself a new home, farther up the mountain, where he believed the air was healthier. Kingsley noted that the move must have suited him, for she found him to be quite healthy and cheerful when they met.

His island also impressed Kingsley. Fernando Po was part of a chain of volcanic islands, and its craters and peaks marked it, in Kingsley's eyes, as "one of the most beautiful [islands] in the world."[34] It was covered with thick forests, but Kingsley lamented the success of Fernando Po's coffee crop, as much of the forest was being cut down and replaced with valuable coffee plantations.

During her visit, Kingsley was more interested in the native population of Fernando Po, the *Bubis*, than by its agriculture or geography. However, even these did not hold her attention for long. She was eager to begin her journey into the French Congo.

In *Travels in West Africa*, Kingsley skips ahead after her descriptions of the Bubis and her observations of Fernando Po, making little mention of how or when she traveled with the MacDonalds back to Calabar or what transpired before her decision to depart for the French Congo in May.

The MacDonalds returned to Calabar with Kingsley in early February, but before she could set out alone again, she decided to remain in Calabar with Lady MacDonald. Upon their return, they learned that an uprising had taken place in the town of Brass about 150 miles away. The uprising was reported in British newspapers as the Brassmen's Revolt. The uprising had been sparked by changes in trade policy and an epidemic of smallpox that swept through Brass, and by the

MARY SLESSOR

While Mary Kingsley was at Calabar, she met a woman who had had an extraordinary impact on life in that part of West Africa. Kingsley traveled to the small village of Ekenge, located in the deep forest between the Cross and Calabar Rivers, to meet the Scottish Presbyterian missionary, Mary Slessor.

Slessor had been living along the coast for nearly 20 years by the time that Kingsley first met her. Slessor was born in Scotland in 1848, and experienced extensive hardship as a child. At the age of 11, she was sent to work in a textile factory; within a short time she was the chief wage earner for her family, working from 6 A.M. until 6 P.M., and helping at home with the housework, including caring for her siblings before and after her long hours at the mill.

Slessor became involved in the activities of the local United Presbyterian Church, which placed a strong emphasis on mission work abroad. She was fascinated by the heroic tales of missionaries traveling to exotic places, setting up missions in India, China, and Calabar. Initially, Slessor's brother planned to enter the mission field, but when he died, Slessor decided to take his place. In 1876, at the age of 28, she set sail for Calabar.

time it ended the Royal Niger Company had been attacked, many of its employees slaughtered, and its goods looted or destroyed. Sir Claude quickly rushed to Brass to do what he could, and his wife and Kingsley remained behind in Calabar.

They were kept busy nursing one patient after another as a typhoid epidemic swept through the region. A makeshift hospital was set up in the MacDonalds' home. The women were quickly exhausted, and it was grim work when many of the patients died, but Kingsley found some humor in the situation when she later related her experiences to her cousin, Rose Kingsley. She told of a patient, delirious with fever, who believed that devils were all around him. He was convinced

Slessor quickly learned the native language of the Calabar people. She traveled from the coast into the interior, and impressed both the natives and visiting Europeans by her ability to tolerate hardships. She drank unfiltered water, slept on the ground, and ate the same food as the natives. She suffered from fever, diarrhea, and other diseases, but continued to work, moving deeper and deeper into the interior to serve new tribes. She became known for her willingness to rescue twins, who were believed by local custom to be cursed. When twins were born, someone generally rushed to alert Slessor, who ran to rescue both the babies and their mother from execution.

By the time Kingsley met her, Slessor was about 46, living in a mud and thatch house, eating native food, and dressed in a simple cotton shift. Her home was full of women and children who had been rescued, as well as many others needing care. She continued to serve for several more years before her death in 1915, and was described by the people she lived among as *Eka Kpukpro Owo* (the "mother of all peoples").

that devils were hiding in the mosquito net around his bed, and for hours, Kingsley attempted to appease him:

> The mosquito curtain after a short time I bodily remove and cast out; then he sees them roosting on his towel horse; remove towel horse. By special request I then take a "quantity of squashy ones" out of the drawers—there are two chests in the room. That done I have to remove seven large devils from beneath the nursing table, "because they are making such a mess bringing up the blood they have been sucking" out of him that he can't take his food. The second night he reported a new devil on top of the wardrobe; he seemed puzzled about it, said it had a "quaint look, rather like his aunt, he fancied." I, dog-tired and sweltering hot and no more intelligent than usual, thought it was one of the usual breed and made a swish at it with a towel while standing on a rickety chair, when hiss, scuffle, flop, down came a great grey brute of a poisonous snake, four foot and more long, which whiffled itself off under the patient's bed: from this position I drove it with a broom on to the verandah, where it escaped down an iron column into the outer darkness. The patient took no interest in it, and on my return I found him engaged in a battle royal with "nine men and two women with drawn swords"; the only thing I could see being a rather strange shaving glass on a pedestal. I took him off this as best I could and whisked him back into bed and held him there until he thought of something else for a wee while. After thirty-six hours he confined his attention to supposing there was a general conspiracy to poison him, and he continued very ill and a considerable nuisance for ten days and nights, at the end of which time he was shipped onto the home-going steamer.[35]

For nearly five weeks, the women nursed typhoid patients, spending many sleepless nights until gradually, by mid-March, the sick had either died or left for home onboard a steamer. Kingsley lingered for several more weeks, hoping that some of the political tension sparked by the uprising would settle. She studied the customs and habits of the local people—the Igbo, Ibibio, and the Effik. She took small boats and paddled along the nearby waterways, collecting specimens of fish and insects.

In one memorable excursion, she wrote of traveling in a canoe accompanied by several men, women, and children. As they traveled along the Cross River, they spotted the corpse of a smallpox victim floating in the water. Kingsley related that her companions paddled hard toward the corpse,

> and then carefully got it alongside the canoe. . . .They then drank calabash after calabash full of water from as close round it as they possibly could squeeze the vessel. . . . "It's a good death charm," they assured me. . . . "Very," said I, "paddle away," for I was fearful that they would drag the putrid thing bodily into the canoe to take home to their less fortunate relations.[36]

Kingsley encountered hippopotamuses and crocodiles during her stay at Calabar. Gradually, rain made it more difficult for her to travel along the Cross River, and she decided to press ahead with her plans. Since politics still prevented her from collecting specimens along the Niger, she decided to explore the Ogooué, instead.

In order to reach the southwest coast by boat, Kingsley was forced to backtrack, as there were no direct shipping routes between Calabar and the southwest. She first headed north to Lagos, and then, with some difficulty, caught a ship for Cameroon and Gabon.

6

Navigating the Ogooué River

Mary Kingsley reached the port city of Glass, a short distance from Libreville, the capital of the French Congo, on May 20, 1895. Gabon lies along the equator, at the center of West Africa. Gabon, at the time of Kingsley's visit, was under the political control of the French, but British traders like John Holt and Hatton and Cookson firmly controlled the territory's economy. Kingsley's plan was to serve as a representative for Hatton and Cookson and to establish a line of credit with them as well as provide them with some goods from her exploration of the territory's interior.

Missionaries were also present in the region, having established small missions along the Ogooué River. These, too, would help Kingsley, who stayed with them during portions of her journey.

It was the world that had not yet been explored or settled that appealed to Kingsley, however. In *Heart of Darkness*, Joseph Conrad gives a glimpse of the pull that many like Kingsley felt when exploring Africa:

> Watching a coast as it slips by the ship is like thinking about an enigma. There it is before you—smiling, frowning, inviting, grand, mean, insipid, or savage, and always mute with an air of whispering—Come and find out.[37]

Kingsley arranged with Hatton and Cookson's representative to trade along the river for about two weeks, after they fruitlessly tried to persuade her that it was too dangerous, and explored the area around Glass and Libreville. She met several members of the *Fang* tribe, and began to learn some basic phrases that would serve her well when she met other Fang during her journey.

Finally, on June 5, 1895, Kingsley joined the other passengers and all-male crew on the small steamer *Mové* and began her journey south to the Ogooué.

Kingsley was pleased with her accommodations on the *Mové*. She had a long, narrow cabin with a bunk located next to the saloon, found the food to be good, and the company enjoyable. The steamer hugged the shore for the first few miles, passing the lighthouse at Point Gombi, which was painted black and white in large, horizontal bands. Unlike many of the lighthouses Kingsley had seen along the West African coast, the Point Gombi lighthouse gave off a steady, reliable beam of light, visible at 17 miles out to sea.

As they pulled away from the lighthouse, the weather grew rougher, and Kingsley noted that many of the suffering African passengers lay on the deck to help combat their seasickness, while the gear from the saloon, which had previously been stowed under seats, slid around them.

Kingsley described the scene that first night:

> The moonlit sea, shimmering and breaking on the dark-ened shore, the black forest and the hills silhouetted against the star-powdered purple sky, and at my feet, the engine-room stoke-hole, lit with the rose colored glow from its furnace, showing by the great wood fire the two nearly naked Krumen [*sic*] stokers, shining like polished bronze in their perspiration, as they throw in on to the fire the billets of red wood that look like freshly-cut chunks of flesh.[38]

It is a vivid scene, but what Kingsley does not mention is how the heat from the nearby furnace, coupled with the climate, must have been sweltering to a woman dressed in full Victorian attire. She seldom devotes any description at all to her own dress, except once praising the value of long skirts when they protected her after falling into a pit. Her ability to adapt to the heat, while dressed for a much chillier English climate, is certainly indication of her physical endurance.

The following day, the *Mové* steamed into the Ogooué River. Kingsley noted an almost immediate change in plant life when they entered the river, from mangrove forests to "a forest rich in bamboo, oil and wine palms" rising up from the "mirror-like brown water."[39] Kingsley could see climbing plants with yellow-, white-, and mauve-colored flowers, red berries, as well as cocoa palms, and smelled a new, intense fragrance. When darkness came, she returned to her cabin, climbed under the mosquito netting, and wrote down impressions of all that she had seen in her journal.

LAMBARÉNÉ

The steamer reached Lambaréné the next day, and there Kingsley was escorted to the Hatton and Cookson factory. Lambaréné, in 20 years, would become the famous site of Albert Schweitzer's hospital, but at the time of Kingsley's visit it was a lush setting of "wild beauty" that she wanted to spend some time enjoying. She was escorted to the porch of the Hatton and Cookson factory accompanied by Mr. Hudson, one of the company's agents, and by Mr. Cockshut, the company's local representative. Her pleasure in the scene quickly vanished when, as Kingsley reports:

> In the twinkling of an eye I am stung all round the neck, and recognise there are lots too [*sic*] many mosquitoes and sandflies in the scenery to permit of contemplation of any kind. Never have I seen sandflies and mosquitoes in such appalling quantities. With a wild ping of joy the latter made for me, and I retired promptly into a dark corner of the verandah, swearing horribly, but internally, and fought them. Mr. Hudson, Agent-general, and Mr. Cockshut, Agent for the Ogowé, walk up and down the beach in front, doubtless talking cargo, apparently unconscious of mosquitoes; but by and by, while we are having dinner, they get their share. I behave exquisitely, and am quite lost in admiration of my own conduct, and busily

deciding in my own mind whether I shall wear one of those plain ring halos, or a solid plate one . . . when Mr. Hudson says in a voice full of reproach to Mr. Cockshut, "You have got mosquitoes here, Mr. Cockshut." Poor Mr. Cockshut doesn't deny it; he has got four on his forehead and his hands are sprinkled with them. . . .

ALBERT SCHWEITZER

Mary Kingsley wrote of her visit to the Jacots at the French mission at Lambaréné. Several years after Kingsley's visit, another European would come to Lambaréné and build a hospital overlooking the Ogooué River. His name was Albert Schweitzer.

Albert Schweitzer was born in 1875 in the small village of Alsace. At the time of Schweitzer's birth, Alsace was part of Germany; today this region is part of France. Schweitzer, the son of a Lutheran pastor, became a skilled organ player as a child, and later became one of the leading experts on organ building. He followed his father's example, studying theology and becoming a professor of theology and philosophy at the University of Strasbourg. He wrote books on theology and biographies of the philosopher Kant, and the composer Bach, as well as books on organ building.

Schweitzer felt a greater calling to serve those less fortunate. By chance, while reading a publication of the Paris Missionary Society, he saw an article describing their desperate need for doctors to serve in the French colony of Gabon. Schweitzer made a dramatic decision: he would give up his professorship and instead return to school, this time as a medical student. Schweitzer's friends and family were all shocked, but in 1905, at the age of 30, Schweitzer began his medical studies.

When his studies were completed, Schweitzer contacted the Paris Missionary Society. To his disappointment, they turned down his offer of his services. Schweitzer was not deterred. While a student, he had married Helene Bresslau, who was a

Mr. Hudson . . . turns to me, and utterly failing to recog-
nise me as a suffering saint, says point blank and savagely,
"You don't seem to feel these things, Miss Kingsley."
Not feel them indeed! Why I could cry over them. Well!
That's all the thanks one gets for trying not to be a
nuisance in this world.[40]

trained nurse. Together, they raised enough funds to cover the
expenses of the hospital they planned to build.

In 1913, the Schweitzers left for Africa. Their destination
was Lambaréné in the French Congo. Initially, Schweitzer
offered medical care in the only structure available: a chicken
coop. Gradually, buildings were added to form a hospital.

It was not an easy life. One year after the Schweitzers
arrived in Africa, World War I broke out. The Schweitzers, as
Germans, were viewed as enemies in French Congo; labeled
prisoners of war, they were sent to a camp in the Pyrenees
Mountains in southern France. When the war ended, the
Schweitzers returned to Alsace, where their daughter was
born. His wife and daughter would remain in Europe when
Schweitzer returned to Africa in 1924.

Schweitzer gradually gained fame for his work in Africa. At
the age of 78, he received the Nobel Prize for his humanitarian
work. He wrote several books, some detailing his life's work,
others expressing his concerns over the development of nuclear
weapons and other topical issues. His often-cited philosophy
of a "reverence for life" never dimmed, and he continued to
work and serve in Africa until his death at Lambaréné at the
age of 90.

The Albert Schweitzer Hospital still serves patients in Lambaréné
in the territory now known as Gabon. It is now administered by
the International Foundation of the Albert Schweitzer Hospital
with the support of the Gabonese Ministry of Health.

Kingsley arranged to stay at the local French mission, the Mission Evangelique. Madame Jacot, the missionary, welcomed her graciously and, in her husband's absence, made Kingsley comfortable in a room normally occupied by the girls who studied at the mission school. The Jacots provided Kingsley with information about the local tribes, including their customs and their language, and she profited from the time with them by collecting specimens of fish and growing more familiar with the region.

Finally, on June 22, she set out again, this time on the steamer *Éclaireur*, where she had a large and comfortable cabin. Kingsley was accompanied by Mr. Cockshut, who was traveling upriver to inspect some of the company's smaller factories, and several other passengers who spoke only French, a language that Kingsley could not speak fluently.

From the deck, Kingsley watched the thick forest slip by, interrupted only occasionally by a small village. The ship would stop frequently at these small villages to discharge passengers. The steamers were greeted by a line of people waiting along the shore, with drums beating and canoes quickly pulling out from shore headed for the steamer. When the canoes reached the ship, passengers on the lower deck (white passengers were housed on the upper deck) climbed over the edge into the rocking canoes and were quickly carried home to the welcoming shouts of their relatives. These were, for the most part, men who had left home to work in one or another of the trading factories; they spent a year in such service before returning home with their goods.

As the Éclaireur traveled up the river, Kingsley noted the patches of *egombie-gombie* trees, whose leaves clustered together at the top, making them look like umbrellas. The trees were strikingly uniform in shape and color, having grown when the inhabitants who had cleared the land moved on to better territory. The current grew stronger as they steamed up the river, and the hills became higher, giving Kingsley the illusion of traveling through a gloomy ravine, surrounded by high cliffs of black, weathered rock. The steamer finally reached the small town of Njole, off Talagouga Island. Kingsley was to be the guest of a young French missionary couple there, the Forgets.

TALAGOUGA

Kingsley enjoyed her time with the Forgets, spending her days hacking her way through the forest and adding to her collection of fish specimens. She learned the tricks of navigating in a dugout canoe, collecting, and trading on short trips away from the mission. She began to plan for the next phase of her journey, which included traveling along the remote region where the Ogooué rapids were found. The Forgets attempted to persuade her not to make the dangerous trip, but she was determined, offering 100 francs to anyone who would lend her a canoe and a crew, and promising the crew a salary plus food. She located a canoe, two English-speaking *Igalwa*, and a crew of six Fang. Just as she was ready to depart, trouble arose: her Fang crew refused to travel above Njole, convinced that they would be killed and eaten by the Fang who lived farther up the river. Finally, Kingsley arranged for two other Igalwa crew members to take the place of the frightened Fang.

The trip seemed doomed from the start. The Forgets nervously pointed out to Kingsley that the majority of her crew members were drunk, and soon after her departure, while seated on a trunk in her canoe, surrounded by her trading box, pillows, sleeping mounts, mosquito netting, and a stick bearing the French flag, it began to rain. When they reached Njole, French officials at first refused to allow Kingsley to proceed, noting that the rapids were too dangerous for a woman traveling without a husband.

Kingsley quickly responded that "neither the Royal Geographical Society's list, in their 'Hints to Travelers,' nor Messrs. Silver, in their elaborate lists of articles necessary for a traveler in tropical climates, make mention of husbands."[41] Kingsley was ultimately allowed to proceed.

Next, she needed *chop* (food) for her crew. She went to three different European trading agents before finally locating one with sufficient fish and beef. Kingsley at last set off, saluted by the trading agent who said goodbye in a "forever tone of voice."[42]

RIDING THE RAPIDS

With a crew, trading goods, and food, Kingsley headed for the *Alemba* rapids. The journey was quite dangerous, and her crew kept as close to the bank as possible, trying to avoid the fastest currents. Frequently they were in danger of crashing into rocks or capsizing, and at those moments M'bo, the man Kingsley had appointed to serve as the head of her crew, would yell to Kingsley, "Jump for bank, sar [*sic*]," and she and most of the crew would jump out and try to cling onto one of the walls of rock and boulder that lined the rapids.[43] Kingsley clung to the rocks as the crew, shouting and pulling, managed to drag the canoe by a chain around to another point, where they would all climb back into the canoe and set off until once more they were forced to scramble out again.

After one violent pitch, they lost most of their poles and paddles, and were forced to fight the rapids with the few they had left. Based on the advice of several natives, they had set their course for a particular village where the residents were thought to be friendly, but they misjudged the distance and so ended up in the thick of night trying to navigate the rapids and find the missing village. They were finally forced to stop, as Kingsley noted:

> For good all-round inconvenience . . . give me going full
> tilt in the dark into the branches of a fallen tree at the
> pace we were going then—and crash, swish, crackle and
> there you are, hung up, with a bough pressing against

your chest, and your hair being torn out and your clothes ribboned by others, while the wicked river is trying to drag away the canoe from under you. After a good hour and more of these experiences, we went hard on to a large black reef of rocks. So firm was the canoe wedged that we in our rather worn-out state couldn't move her so we wisely decided to "lef em" and see what could be done towards getting food and a fire for the remainder of the night.[44]

Wading to shore, they stumbled in the dark until M'bo finally spotted the light from fires, and soon they could hear drumbeats in the distance. They came upon a tiny village of palm mat huts and several small fires, around which villagers were dancing. The villagers welcomed the travelers, and Kingsley was given the use of a small shelter, whose right-hand side was open and part of the roof was covered with palm branches. Kingsley ate quickly and then guarded their cargo while her crew ate. Then she followed a slippery path to the shore, where she was struck by the beauty of the mountains, rising out of clouds of silver-grey mist, and the sight of thousands of fireflies flickering over the white foam of the rapids.

It is at this moment in *Travels in West Africa* that Kingsley gives a brief glimpse of what drew her to Africa, and of why she seldom was at peace in England:

> The majesty and beauty of the scene fascinated me, and I stood leaning with my back against a rock pinnacle watching it. Do not imagine it gave rise, in what I am pleased to call my mind, to those complicated, poetical reflections natural beauty seems to bring out in other people's minds. It never works that way with me; I just lose all sense of human individuality, all memory of human life, with its grief and worry and doubt, and become part of the atmosphere.[45]

After returning to her makeshift shelter, Kingsley spent a restless night. Rats swarmed among the huts, and at one point, having nodded off, Kingsley awoke with a start to discover that she had fallen out of the house and was lying on the ground.

The next day she pressed on, fighting whirlpools and rapids, passing caves that she refused to explore, admitting to fearing them. They traveled on to the mouth of the Okana River. They landed on the island of Kondo Kondo, where they made camp for the night. The island was covered with sand, interrupted by slabs of polished rock, and in between the rocks, Kingsley was astonished to find thousands of white lilies. Kingsley picked one and sent it in a letter to Charles Günther, noting that it had been described to her as the "lily of the spirit of the rapids." That lily and the letter Kingsley wrote are now on display in the National History Museum in Kensington, England.[46]

Kingsley and her crew braved the Alemba rapids, and then made the dangerous journey back to Talagouga. Kingsley did not intend to remain long with the Jacots. She was already planning her next journey: this one on foot through the territory that lay between the Remboué and Ogooué rivers. She planned to hike through rain forests, swamps, and rocky hills between the rivers, territory no European had visited before, collecting specimens as she went.

The Jacots once more attempted to dissuade her from the journey, but Kingsley was determined. She obtained the goods she would need to trade along her journey, managed to get permission from the French officials overseeing the territory, and packed her belongings: her blouses and woolen skirts in her black waterproof bag, her papers, trade tobacco, and geological specimens in her case, and her brush, comb, and toothbrush in "a basket constructed for catching human souls . . . given . . . as a farewell gift by a valued friend, a witch doctor."[47]

Finally, with the help of Jacot, Kingsley assembled her crew: a Galoa named Ngouta, who was hired as an interpreter but whose only English seemed to be "P'raps," "Tis better so," and "Lordy, Lordy, helpee me"; four Adjoumba who Kingsley nicknamed "Gray Shirt," "Singlet," "Silent," and "Pagan"; and one additional Adjoumba, nicknamed "Passenger," who was not a paid crew member but had simply decided to come along for the fun of it.[48]

PREPARING FOR THE JOURNEY

While Kingsley prepared for her next journey, she spent any additional time at Talagouga practicing her canoeing and gathering specimens. She became quite skilled at maneuvering the dugout canoe, noting that "I can honestly and truly say that there are only two things I am proud of—one is that Doctor Günther has approved of my fishes, and the other is that I can paddle an Ogowé canoe."[49]

Kingsley also deepened her knowledge of native customs and trade practices, all of which she hoped to use during the next phase of her travels. She noted that all payment along the Ogooué was made in trade goods, rather than in coins. High value was placed on certain goods, such as gunpowder, tobacco, and rum.

Kingsley was unimpressed by the native diet, which consisted largely of plantains (a fruit similar to bananas) and manioc (a starchy, edible root). Kingsley noted that the sweet, non-poisonous manioc, from which tapioca is derived, was seldom cultivated; she found a more common manioc whose large roots were soaked in water in an attempt to remove the poison, then dried and grated, or beaten into dough in a large wooden trough resembling a canoe. The thumping sound of the manioc being beaten into dough was a sound that Kingsley heard often in the villages surrounding Talagouga.

The dough was used to thicken broth, or wrapped in plantain leaves, steamed, and then cooked over a wood fire.

"It is a good food when it is properly prepared," Kingsley noted, "but when a village has soaked its soil-laden manioc tubers in one and the same pool of water for years, the water in that pool becomes a trifle strong, and both it and the manioc get a smell which once smelt is never to be forgotten. . . ."[50]

In addition to manioc, villagers ate dried fish, which Kingsley says was appropriately called "stink-fish", and snails. The smoked meat Kingsley encountered is she memorably described as:

> . . . badly prepared, just hung up in the smoke of the fires, which hardens it, blackening the outside quickly; but when the lumps are taken out of the smoke, in a short time cracks occur in them, and the interior part proceeds to go bad, and needless to say maggoty. If it is kept in the smoke, as it often is to keep it out of the way of dogs and driver ants, it acquires the toothsome taste and texture of a piece of old tarpaulin.[51]

Kingsley blamed the bland, tasteless diet for various intestinal diseases and vision problems, and hinted that perhaps the missionaries might better focus their attention on teaching cooking and more useful skills, rather than attempting to eradicate the local customs of polygamy.

In fact, in her attitude toward polygamy, which was one of the focuses of missionary fervor, Kingsley demonstrates a surprisingly enlightened attitude, noting that many men adopted it simply to provide them with enough to eat. This was particularly true of the Fang, who ate meals throughout the day, even when they were hunting. She noted the difficulty of one woman being able to carry out all of the work necessary, including childcare, meal preparation, rubber cultivation and the process of selling it at the market, carrying water each day from the stream, and cultivating the crops. The practice of polygamy also ensured that no woman or her children were alone and uncared for, and indeed Kingsley's single-state caused great astonishment among many she encountered.

Once, while paddling near the beach of Kangwe, Kingsley struggled to make her way back against the current. A man who introduced himself as Samuel and described himself as "a very good man" offered to paddle her back to the mission. He and his wife climbed into the canoe with Kingsley, and Samuel, who knew a fair amount of English, quickly began to pepper Kingsley with questions:

> "You be Christian, ma?" said he. I asked him if he had ever met a white man who was not. "Yes, ma," says Samuel. I said "You must have been associating with people whom you ought not to know." Samuel fortunately not having a repartee for this, paddled on with his long paddle for a few seconds. "Where be your husband, ma?" was the next conversational bomb he hurled at me. "I no got one," I answer. "No got," says Samuel, paralysed with astonishment; and as Mrs. S., who did not know English, gave one of her vigorous drives with her paddle at this moment, Samuel as near as possible got jerked head first into the Ogowé, and we took on board about two bucketsful of water. He recovered himself, however and returned to his charge. "No got one, ma?" "No," say I furiously. "Do you get much rubber round here?" "I no be trade man," says Samuel, refusing to fall into my trap for changing conversation. "Why you no got one?" The remainder of the conversation is unreportable.[52]

Finally, Kingsley's preparations were complete and she was ready to set off on a new adventure. On July 22, 1895, the day of her departure, Kingsley awoke with a terrible headache, a sign that she was about to suffer a case of malaria.[53] Rain was pouring down, and her crew was late, but Kingsley was not going to be delayed. She was eager to be off on the next phase of her journey.

7

Reaching
the Rembwé

Kingsley and her crew waited until early afternoon, but neither her headache nor the rain passed. At last, she determined to press ahead. Her luggage was stowed into a canoe, and she lay in the middle of it for about an hour, waiting for her headache to stop.

In a lecture, Kingsley outlined the perils and benefits of such travel by dugout canoe:

> When you have to get into one it strikes you as insecure, and insecure it is if you neither know how to use it or sit in it. Moreover, you at first object to sitting in the lot of dirty water that it contains, but you soon get over this, philosophically recognising that the chances are you will soon be out of it into cleaner water, and after that you may not require a canoe again, what with sharks or crocodiles, &c., and the chances of simple drowning. Yet that canoe is also full of good points, and when you get used to it, you see you can go through surf it in you could not in a white man's boat, and that on rivers and swamps you can go in it where you could go in no other craft; while for comfort, when outside circumstances are reasonable, there is no form of boat half so pleasant; the rapid, gliding motion of a well-addled canoe is something more than comfort, it is a keen physical pleasure.[54]

Gradually, as her headache lessened, Kingsley was able to sit up and look about her. They paused briefly at Igalway, south of Lambaréné, to load up with yam and plantain supplies, and then set off again, being periodically greeted by other canoers who asked their destination and expressed their astonishment at the choice of Rembwé. Their travel was frequently interrupted by sandbars, requiring the crew to stop, unload some of the cargo to lighten the canoes, push them off the sandbar, load the cargo up again, and then paddle along until the next sandbar.

They reached Arevooma, where Kingsley was hosted by her crew member, Gray Shirt, and his wife at their home of split bamboo with a palm thatched roof. The home had a single room, with a table and chair set on its porch, where Kingsley had tea while screened off from the curious eyes of the village's inhabitants by a calico sheet. Then, still battling her headache, Kingsley was forced to attend a religious service, held by three of her crew who were Christians. They sang hymns while being attacked by mosquitoes, and Kingsley (not the most religious woman under the best of circumstances) suffered through the lengthy service.

At last, Kingsley was escorted—through thick clouds of mosquitoes—back to her host's home, where she quickly climbed into bed, noting that she first needed to carefully sweep all of the mosquitoes from under the mosquito netting around the bed and let in the family's cat, who was scratching at the door. As soon as she took off her boots, she put on slippers—"for it never does in this country to leave off boots altogether at any time and risk getting bitten by mosquitoes on the feet, when you are on the march," Kingsley notes, "because the rub of your boot on the bite always produces a sore, and a sore when it comes in the Gorilla country, comes to stay." [55] Kingsley fell asleep to the noise of the cat jumping out from under the mosquito net to chase rats, killing them to the sound of squeals and loud meows, and then jumping back on the bed until she heard another rat.

Kingsley's awakening was not much quieter, coming at dawn with a loud knocking at her door—loud enough to cause two large centipedes and a scorpion to fall down on her bed from their hiding place in the mosquito net. Kingsley learned that another villager was eager to join their expedition, a man who wanted to travel to a trading factory on the Rembwé but had hesitated to make the trip alone from fear of being attacked by the Fang tribesmen.

Kingsley was concerned at the clear fear the man demonstrated at the thought of the Fang, for her own expedition would be traveling through that very stretch of territory. She was somewhat reassured when one of her crew, Pagan, explained that he knew two Fang tribesmen who live on an island in Lake Ncovi who he thought might be friendly. The expedition determined to press ahead toward Lake Ncovi in search of the hopefully friendly Fang. They traveled armed with rifles, which were tied onto Kingsley's baggage. The flint-locks were covered with sheaths made of black-haired gorilla skin or leopard skin.

ALONG THE RIVERBANK

The expedition set out, aided by a strong current, and passed a series of canoes laden with fruit and other trade goods heading the opposite way. Kingsley found the forest on either side of the river banks lovely, noting that climbing plants spread out over trees that had been struck by lightning, creating an illusion "as if some one had spread a great green coverlet over the forest so as to keep it dry."[56] Kingsley was lulled by the rhythm of the crew, swinging their long, red wooden paddles, until they struck the occasional sandbar and needed to pile out, push, and climb back in.

The river became wider, and the forest on either side was sprinkled with bright red and yellow flowers. At various points, they could see tunnels carved into the forest, marking the path to one village or another. They passed into a new river—the Karkola River—and briefly stopped. Kingsley had tea and then explored the riverbank, where she found a species of beautiful small fish marked by a black stripe on either side of their tales—fish so tame that they would eat crumbs from her hand. Then she and her crew set off again.

The Karkola grew wider and deeper, marked by forest on its east bank and low shrubbery on its west. The current began to move faster, and the eastern bank gradually changed from clay to sand. They had entered Fang territory, a fact noted by her crew with some alarm.

Hippos appeared on one side of the riverbank, lumbering towards them, and so the crew quickly paddled over to the other side, where they were greeted by a large number of crocodiles, resting on the sand. The crew paddled even faster, carrying them through a channel and into a lake, Lake Ncovi:

> It is exceedingly beautiful. The rich, golden sunlight of the late afternoon soon followed by the short-lived, glorious flushes of color of the sunset and the after-glow, play over the scene as we paddle across the lake to the N.N.E.—our canoe leaving a long trail of frosted silver behind her as she glides over the mirror-like water, and each stroke of the paddle sending down air with it to come up again in luminous silver bubbles.[57]

Despite the beauty around her, Kingsley felt uneasy on the lake. They reached an island, where they could hear the noise of shouting coming from a nearby village. Kingsley's men put away their paddles and picked up their loaded guns. They quickly attracted the notice of the Fang villagers, who surrounded them, all armed (men and women) with guns and knives, all preparing for a fight.

Pagan and Gray Shirt quickly began shouting the name of the person they knew who they believed lived in that village, while Kingsley offered what she hoped was a casual greeting to the angry faces. After several unpleasant minutes, a middle-aged man appeared and turned out to be the hoped-for friend. Gradually, the Fang crowd was transformed from hostile to eager, and Kingsley was led into the village to be surrounded by even more people and their dogs, where she witnessed this memorable scene:

> Every child in the place as soon as it saw my white face let a howl . . . and fled into the nearest hut, headlong, and I fear, from the continuance of the screams, had fits.

The town was exceedingly filthy—the remains of the crocodile they had been eating the week before last, and piles of fish offal, and remains of an elephant, hippo, or manatee—I really can't say which, decomposition was too far advanced—united to form a most impressive stench.[58]

The village contained three streets, rather than the usual single main road, and was lined with bark huts. Kingsley asked her crewmember, Ajumba, to explain that they needed a place to stay for the night and hoped that three Fang would join them to lead them to the Rembwé. This sparked an intense discussion, accompanied by vivid gestures, which lasted nearly two hours. Finally, she was led to a hut, the crowd drawing back only slightly to let Kingsley pass before following her. Kingsley was as tall as the hut's roof, and had to stoop to get in through the door.

The hut was windowless and only about 14 square feet. The floor was sand, and the bed offered to Kingsley was really a rough wooden bench with a few dirty cloths on top of it, and a block of wood to serve as a pillow. The hut had no other furniture.

Kingsley had tea inside the hut, while a crowd of faces watched her from the doorway. Her crew arranged to add three Fang to join the expedition; three being the most they felt could safely be added to the crew. The reputation of the Fang was that they would kill the black traders who ventured into their country, slice them into pieces, eat a portion, and then smoke the rest for later.[59] None of her crew knew the exact route they needed to take, but the Fang did know how to get to a village called Efoua, a place where no white trader had ever been. They knew that the Efoua people traveled along the Rembwé with their goods, so they reasoned that a route to the Rembwé must exist from Efoua.

Kingsley then attempted to sleep, but mosquitoes and lice quickly made that impossible. She crept out to the river, and borrowing a canoe and paddle, pushed off into the dark lake. She paddled to a far bank, where she found five hippos eating. She headed off again in another direction, reaching a small rocky bay lined with a thin patch of sand. Far from anyone, she decided to take a quick bath, and then returned to her hut to wait for dawn. The expedition set off at 5:30 A.M., paddling for several hours before reaching a slimy marsh through which they would begin to travel on land.

THROUGH THE FOREST

The land journey was much more tiring, leaving Kingsley frequently too exhausted to make any kind of detailed notes in her journal. There were no paths through the forest, and Kingsley discovered that the Fang were much faster marchers than the Ajumba, who were more skilled at paddling the canoe. Because the Fang frequently stopped to eat, the crew soon sorted out a plan: The Fang marched ahead, then when they stopped for a snack every two hours, the others would catch up with them. Kingsley would rest for a few minutes and then set out ahead, giving herself a bit of a head start before the others caught up and then passed her.

During one of these stretches, when Kingsley had gone on ahead of the others, she discovered, down in a muddy ravine, a herd of five elephants. While a picturesque sight, elephants posed a real danger. They could charge the unwary explorer, but Kingsley had been told to quickly hide behind trees and move down wind so that the elephants could neither see nor smell her. This she did, observing them from a safe distance as they washed themselves in the muddy water.

The elephants had left huge, muddy footprints along the trail, and this created a problem for Kingsley and her crew. The path was completely covered with huge footprints, which had created a series of small ponds, interrupted by patches of slippery mud. The crew was soon stumbling and sliding through the mud, falling often. When she reached the other side of the ravine, Kingsley noticed that her crew were examining themselves, and she soon discovered why:

> Before I joined them [I] felt a fearful pricking irritation. Investigation of the affected part showed a tick of terrific size with its head embedded in the flesh, pursuing this interesting subject, I found three more, and had awfully hard work to get them off and painful too for they give one not only a feeling of irritation at their holding-on place, but a streak of rheumatic-feeling pain up from it.[60]

Having pulled off the elephant ticks, the crew pressed forward, into more mountainous, rocky country, with forests of huge, gray-white trees, 100 feet tall, whose boughs formed an arching canopy above that blocked out the sunlight.

Soon, they found a cluster of five gorillas, chattering and moving among the trees. Kingsley and her crew watched them for several minutes until one of Kingsley's crew unexpectedly gave out a loud sneeze, startling the gorillas and sending them back into the forest.

The first day's march proved the easiest, although it was also the longest, some 25 miles. Late in the afternoon, Kingsley—having walked ahead again—suddenly fell into a 15-foot-deep pit, landing on a pile of spikes. Kingsley noted how glad she was to have worn clothes better suited to England:

> It is at these times you realise the blessing of a good thick skirt. Had I paid heed to the advice of many people in England, who ought to have known better, and did not do it themselves, and adopted masculine garments, I should have been spiked to the bone, and done for. Whereas, save for a good many bruises, here I was with the fulness of my skirt tucked under me, sitting on nine ebony spikes some twelve inches long, in comparative comfort, howling lustily to be hauled out.[61]

After some time, Kingsley was pulled out by rope, and she proceeded to Efoua. There, Kingsley was surrounded by curious villagers before being led to the hut of the village chief—a hut with two rooms empty except for a few boxes, a fire on the floor, some small bags hanging from the roof poles, and a large number of insects. Kingsley was introduced as a trader, and she soon was purchasing rubber balls, elephant-hair necklaces, and some spoons.

The hut was surrounded by curious villagers, who crowded around her door and pressed their eyes against the cracks in the hut's walls. Soon, Kingsley heard new holes being drilled into the walls of the hut to allow more villagers to peer in at her.

Exhausted, she settled herself in among some boxes and her own cargo, and resting her head on the sack of tobacco she had brought, she slept briefly before awakening to a terrible smell in the hut. She traced it to the bags hanging from the roof poles:

> So I took down the biggest one, and carefully noted exactly how the tie-tie had been put round its mouth; for these things are important and often mean a lot. I then shook its contents out in my hat, for fear of losing anything of value. They were a human hand, three big toes, four eyes, two ears, and other portions of the human frame. The hand was fresh, the others only so so, and shriveled.[62]

SWAMP MARCH

Leaving Efoua, the expedition proceeded, marching along high hills interrupted by deep ravines, each with a watery swamp at its base. Whoever was in front at the time they came to a swamp was charged with finding the best way to cross it; at times this fell to Kingsley, who was unwilling to demonstrate any kind of weakness or fear in front of her men. There was little safe (in other words, boiled) water available, and the journey was hot and thirsty work. Many of the villages they came upon had dangerous reputations, and so there was little they could do except keep walking.

Finally, they stopped at the village of Egaja, which had a similarly dangerous reputation but was the only stopping point along their journey. There, Kingsley greeted the chief by announcing that she had heard that his town was a "thief town," and when the chief protested Kingsley challenged him to prove otherwise. He immediately welcomed her very graciously, offering her his own relatively spacious hut. The town had never seen a white person before, and the chief soon brought his mother to Kingsley, hoping that she could care for his mother's ulcerous arm.

Once Kingsley had cleaned and bandaged the woman's arm, other villagers began appearing, hoping that Kingsley could cure them of their sicknesses or ailments. It was several hours before Kingsley completed her nursing and was able to briefly rest, before being called upon to rescue one of her crew, who was in debt to one of the men in the village and was in danger of being killed. Kingsley rescued the crew member and briefly went back to bed before the expedition set out again.

THE PATH TO REMBWÉ

Kingsley's goal of reaching the "Big River," as the Rembwé was known, led her through rubber plantations and more swamps. One swamp took more than two hours to cross; Kingsley went in over her head twice and emerged at the end with a circle of leeches around her neck and more on her hands. Finally, they reached the muddy black water of the Rembwé. Kingsley was about an hour south of her intended arrival point, a trading post operated by the British agents Hatton and Cookson.

A message was sent to the head of the trading factory, who arrived shortly after and transported Kingsley and her crew up the river. There Kingsley was able to satisfactorily pay her crew for their work, and say her farewells.

BACK TO THE COAST

Kingsley stayed for several days at Agonjo as the guest of the British trading agent, Mr. Sanga Glass, who helped arrange transportation down the Rembwé for her return to the coast. Mr. Glass located a bush and river trader known both as Obanjo and Captain Johnson, who had a canoe large enough to accommodate Kingsley and her gear, although it was incomplete and used a quilt for a sail. A few bamboo poles created a kind of shelter on one end of the boat, and it was on this rather rickety perch that Kingsley sat, or rather reclined, rolling off frequently when the boat would pitch.

The trip was almost unbearably slow, with Captain Johnson choosing to drop anchor for the night only five miles from their starting point. Kingsley offered to navigate, and she was left with a good share of the steering for the four days it took them to travel down the Rembwé. Captain Johnson attempted to persuade Kingsley to travel on with him, into the Spanish territory north of French Congo. He promised to show her "plenty country, plenty men, elephants, leopards, gorillas."[63] Kingsley had seen enough men, elephants, leopards, and gorillas, and was ready to reach Glass.

As the canoe pulled into the port, Kingsley was greeted by the British agent Mr. Hudson, who had heard of her dangerous journey and had been so anxious for her safety that he had sent another canoe after her, which had missed her while she was traveling. It had been an incredible journey, and one that Kingsley vowed to repeat again some day.

EXPLORING CORSICO

After resting for a few days in Glass, Kingsley traveled on to the island of Corsico, about 20 miles from Gabon. Kingsley had been told that there were several freshwater lakes in the middle of the island, from which she might find several interesting species of fish. Kingsley made the trip in a single day, and was welcomed as a guest at the Presbyterian mission there.

Kingsley thoroughly explored the tiny island for two days, waiting for an expedition to collect fish to be organized. At last, on August 7, she and several of the island women set out. When they finally began collecting fish, Kingsley was disappointed to find that they were all the common African mudfish, a species of no interest to her. "But there! It's Africa all over; presenting one with familiar objects when one least requires them," Kingsley wrote,

> ... and unfamiliar, such as elephants and buffalos when you are out for a quiet stroll armed with a butterfly net, to say nothing of snakes in one's bed and scorpions in one's boots. One's view of life gets quite distorted; I don't believe I should be the least surprised to see a herd of hippo stroll on to the line out of one of the railway tunnels at Notting Hill Gate station [in England]. West Africa is undoubtedly bad for one's mind.[64]

Kingsley traveled on to Libreville, where she collected butterfly specimens and made notes on what she had seen during her travels. In mid-September, she boarded the *Niger* and traveled north to German-controlled Cameroon. There, sailing to the town of Victoria, Kingsley gazed upon the 13,000-foot-high Mount Cameroon, what she called "my great temptation—the magnificent *Mungo Mah Lobeh* (the Throne of Thunder)."[65]

Kingsley had seen the huge mountain—the highest in West Africa—several times before. This time, she decided to climb it. On September 20, 1895, she left Victoria in the early morning. A German official helped arrange for several experienced guides and carriers to accompany Kingsley. The weather was clear when they left, but as soon as they reached the foothills of the mountain, it began to rain. By the time they reached shelter late in the afternoon, Kingsley was soaked and chilled and, coming upon a Swiss-run mission, they decide to make camp for the night. Kingsley's hut was quickly surrounded by curious Africans and faces poked through her window until she respectfully announced that "the circus is closed for repairs" and closed the shutters. She created a makeshift pillow by wrapping the missionaries' German and English bibles and

KINGSLEY THE ICHTHYOLOGIST

When Mary Kingsley returned from her second trip to West Africa, she brought with her specimens from 65 species of fish and 18 species of reptile. She had kept her promise to Albert Günther to provide the British Museum with freshwater specimens from various points of her travels, and Günther published the details of her discoveries—18 of which had never before been collected from the Gabon territory, and seven of which had never before been seen by scientists—in an article in *Annals and Magazine of Natural History* in 1896, entitled "Report on a collection of reptiles and fishes made by Miss M. H. Kingsley during her travels on the Ogowe River and in Old Calabar."

Her collection represented a major contribution to the field of ichthyology, and to honor her work, Günther named three of the species of fish for Kingsley: *Brycinus kingsleyae, Brienomyrus kingsleyae,* and *Ctenopoma kingsleyae.* Kingsley became best known for her writings on African culture and religious practices, but her contributions to ichthyology continued to inspire scientists long after her death.

To mark the centennial of her trip to West Africa, an expedition was cosponsored by the National Geographic Society, the National Science Foundation, the American Museum of Natural History, and the Wildlife Conservation Society. An international team of biologists traveled to the Ogooué River basin in Gabon to continue the work begun by Kingsley. Their goals were to collect and catalog the freshwater fish they found in the basin, to establish a reference museum and library in Gabon, and train students in field methods and ecological assessment.

two hymnbooks in a pair of their trousers and tried to sleep, with little success.

On the next day, it was raining heavily again, and the narrow path was slippery and muddy. The expedition traveled cautiously up the path in single file, slipping and falling often. Kingsley occasionally paused at a few pools to collect specimens, but noted that the surroundings were much better suited for a botanist, rich as they were in exotic plant life. At last, they came to a rushing river, where Kingsley found a group of Africans washing their clothes. Kingsley joined them, trying to wash the mud out of her skirts, before reaching a small German military post. Kingsley was welcomed by the German officer in charge, who took one look at her and quickly suggested a hot bath. This Kingsley refused, noting: "Men can be trying! How in the world is any one going to take a bath in the house with no doors, and only very sketchy wooden window-shutters?" [66]

Kingsley spent the night in the officer's makeshift home, and then set out again before dawn. The paths were still wet and muddy, and it continued to pour. They made camp on a side of the mountain, fighting heavy rain as they tried to set up cots and tents.

The next day, the weather having finally cleared, they continued their climb. Suddenly, Kingsley's crew informed her that they had no more water, and so would need to turn back. Kingsley was furious, but rather than turn back she sent a messenger down the mountain to the German officer, asking him to send up some supplies of water. At last, the water arrived, and Kingsley explored the mountain face alone.

The weather finally cleared, and the strong sun posed another hazard: Kingsley's face and mouth were quickly covered with blisters, some of them bleeding. Kingsley was forced to send down for more water, and food supplies, before it once again began to rain heavily. Because water supplies were so scarce, Kingsley decided to guard the water—and rum—

herself, placing them around her bed. Each time the rain stopped a large cloud of bees descended, targeting the rum. Then came spiny beetles, which held onto her blankets and hissed at her when she tried to remove them.

As the team climbed higher, the rain was accompanied by cold winds. The mist was so thick that they could see little ahead of them. Kingsley's crew wanted to turn back, but she pushed forward, finding shelter under trees and creating makeshift coverings. As the rain continued, Kingsley debated giving up the attempt to reach the mountain's summit, but she was reluctant to turn back after coming so far. She finally asked for volunteers among her men, and two agreed to accompany her.

Finally, on September 26, she reached the peak, climbing through mist, strong winds, and stinging rain. She discovered the peak almost by accident, peering through the fog until she had found what she decided was the highest point. She found several empty bottles scattered on the ground, left—she guessed—by German officers who had reached the peak before her.

It was almost anticlimactic after the dangerous ascent. Kingsley took a few specimens, then placed her card beneath a small cluster of rocks—a gesture of respect to the mountain, she wrote, but no doubt also a way to mark her accomplishment: the first white woman to ascend Mount Cameroon. Kingsley wrote,

> Verily I am no mountaineer, for there is in me no exultation, but only a deep disgust because the weather has robbed me of my main object in coming here, namely to get a good view and an idea of the way the unexplored mountain range behind Calabar trends. I took my chance and it failed, so there's nothing to complain about.[67]

Kingsley and her guides made the dangerous descent, reaching the German post late on September 27. Once more, the German officer suggested a hot bath; once more Kingsley refused. The next day she returned to Victoria. One final adventure awaited: the rain had created new, rushing streams of water and waterfalls that blocked their path at several points. Kingsley's guides were alarmed, but gradually, wading through chest-high water, teams of two men carried each small load of gear until everything was once more on the path. They were forced to repeat the process five times before reaching Victoria, just after nightfall.

Here, Kingsley ends *Travels in West Africa.* She was once more safe, comfortable, warm, and well fed. She was suffering from a terrible cold, but was not ready to sleep:

> As I sat on the verandah overlooking Victoria and the sea, in the dim soft light of the stars, with the fire-flies round me, and the lights of Victoria way below, and heard the soft rush of the Lukola River, and the sound of the sea-surf on the rocks, and the tom-tomming [*sic*] and singing of the natives, all matching and mingling together, "Why did I come to Africa?" thought I. Why! Who would not come to its twin brother Hell itself for all the beauty and the charm of it![68]

8

The Final Journey

Kingsley returned to England on November 30, 1895. It was a cold, grey evening when her ship pulled into port at Liverpool. Kingsley brought with her a small monkey. Stories of her travels had preceded her, and she was met at the dock by a journalist. Her publisher, George Macmillan, had ensured that Kingsley's adventures received plenty of press, and her return home was an occasion, marking a new period of celebrity for her.

Many of the stories published upon Kingsley's return contained only scraps of truth, interspersed with sensational accounts purporting to reveal all that she had seen and found in West Africa. While many told outrageous stories of encounters with cannibals and gorillas, the one that Kingsley felt compelled to object to was published in the *Daily Telegraph*. In it, the newspaper praised Kingsley and described her as representative of a "new woman":

> Yes! Anything seems possible in Africa, yet almost more wonderful than the hidden marvels of that Dark Continent are the qualities of heart and mind which could carry a lovely English lady through such experiences as Miss Kingsley has "manfully borne."[69]

Kingsley quickly issued a response to this article, noting that she had been heavily dependent on many men for the success of her expedition and that she flatly rejected any description of herself as a "new woman": "I just paddled round obscure corners and immersed myself in catastrophes."[70]

Kingsley's brother, Charley, was still traveling in Singapore when she returned, so she busied herself sorting through the large numbers of specimens she had brought back, and reliving her experiences by writing them down. In January 1896, she was invited to give a lecture before the Scottish Geographical Society. She quickly discovered a new talent; she was a lively and interesting speaker, and soon she was lecturing before many different groups. While Kingsley was uncomfortable in social situations, she found lectures to be quite different; they offered a structured gathering where she had a specific role to play, and information to share.

Her brother returned to England in June. By then, Kingsley was busy putting the final touches on the manuscript that would become *Travels in West Africa*. For most of the year after her return from Africa, she was busy lecturing, writing, and helping her brother. Her book was published on January 21, 1897. It quickly became a best seller. The reviews were full of praise, and the invitations to Kingsley to speak increased.

Kingsley began to long to return to Africa. She arranged to leave England as soon as her brother left on another trip. Her brother became ill, however, and Kingsley was forced to postpone her own plans, first to nurse him, and then to accompany him on a trip to Wales in the hope that the change in climate and scenery would be good for him.

It was a depressing time for Kingsley. Once more, she was isolated and forced to care for a sick family member at a time when she wanted to be far from England. She wrote to a friend, "It is just as if the old days were coming back."[71]

If Kingsley could not go to Africa, she determined to again write about it. The new book would become *West African Studies*, and into it, Kingsley put much of the material written long ago for *The Bights of Benin*, some material that she had edited out of *Travels in West Africa*, and portions of her lectures. In the manuscript, she also offered her thoughts on how best West Africa could be governed and administered.

She spent much of 1897 lecturing, caring for her brother, and working on *West African Studies*. Late in the year, Kingsley herself became ill, and after a lecture tour in Ireland, she suffered a particularly bad attack of influenza, coming close to death before slowly recovering.

By mid-1898, Kingsley and her brother decided to move from their tiny, dark apartment to a small house about a mile away. The move was a mark of Kingsley's new financial success. Of course, her nail-covered statue went with her, greeting guests from a position of honor in the entranceway. She continued to lecture, to work on *West African Studies*, and to care for her brother. When Charley announced that he was planning to travel to China, Kingsley felt a spark of hope, planning to set off for West Africa as soon as he left. In late 1898, Kingsley once more suffered an attack of influenza, all the while caring for friends and neighbors who were suffering from their own physical and mental ailments.

CELEBRATED AUTHOR

West African Studies was finally published on January 31, 1899. The reviews praised Kingsley's knowledge, complemented her fresh writing style, although some noted that the material was too basic for scientists, but too sophisticated for the public. Nonetheless, the book sold well.

Kingsley continued to write and lecture, making plans for a return trip to West Africa, this time to the center of the Congo. Her brother created a new problem when he announced a desire to travel with her, trouble since, as Kingsley explained to a friend, "he is only fit to travel in savage countries where people can get about comfortably." She was able to convince him not to make the trip, and then was forced to remain in England with him until he had found a new destination.

As Kingsley planned and then postponed her return to West Africa, however, a crisis broke out in South Africa. British and Boer forces were battling for control of the Transvaal and its rich store of gold and diamonds.

Kingsley had been lecturing on behalf of the Colonial Nursing Association for some time, urging that male and female nurses be sent to West Africa and work on hospital ships to provide care. As it became clear that nurses would be desperately needed to care for the sick and wounded in South Africa, Kingsley decided to volunteer to serve.

Her first offer was turned down, but by mid-February 1900, Kingsley's offer was accepted. She made preparations to depart for Cape Town, planning to serve there and then travel on to her "real" destination: West Africa.

SOUTH AFRICA

Kingsley traveled to Cape Town on a military transport ship, loaded down with more then 600 soldiers and other military personnel. Because so many men and supplies were crammed on board the ship, the conditions were horrific, sanitation was poor, there were not enough toilets, and not enough water. Quickly, soldiers began to fall sick. As the ship traveled further south, more soldiers, dressed in uniforms of thick flannel shirts and woolen pants, began to suffer and grow ill.

THE BOER WAR

As the nineteenth century ended, British attempts at imperialism in South Africa led to the Boer War. British forces, seeking to dominate the African continent, determined to extend their control of South Africa by seizing the Boer republics of the Transvaal and the Orange Free State, two territories that were rich in gold mines.

A deterioration of diplomatic relations, sparked by debates over access to mining rights and the granting of monopolies, as well as an attempt to overthrow the government in Transvaal, led to a crisis when additional British troops were sent into South Africa and refused to leave. War broke out in October 1899, when Boer forces, hoping to gain the initiative, seized British-held territory. Britain had planned for an offensive operation, but quickly found its troops on the defensive, attempting to free captured cities.

British forces finally turned the tide, capturing the capital cities of Transvaal and the Orange Free State in May and June of 1900. With these decisive victories, the British government

Kingsley was called into service, beginning to care for sick soldiers before they had even sailed close to South Africa. They finally reached Cape Town on March 28, and Kingsley was given an unpleasant assignment: not to nurse British soldiers, but instead to care for the sick and wounded Boer prisoners-of-war, who were being interned in an old barracks in Simonstown, on the other side of the African peninsula from the Cape of Good Hope.

While the town was pleasant, the makeshift hospital was not. Wards had been created in the larger rooms of the former barracks, but they were in desperate need of repair. Paint was peeling from the walls, and the narrow beds were covered only with sheets made from rough cloth normally used for sacks. The hospital contained more than 200 patients and, when

believed the war was won. Boer forces hid in the bush country and engaged in guerilla warfare for the next two years, successfully ambushing British troops with their tactics. British forces, long used to operating from a position of strength against inferior powers in quick and decisive wars, suddenly found themselves fighting a very different kind of war, and one that their training had not prepared them for.

Finally, British forces switched to fighting the Boer way, using guerilla tactics and gradually succeeding by brutal methods: burning farms and seizing food in the countryside to prevent it from being used by the Boers; capturing Boer women and children, labeling them "collaborators," and imprisoning them in concentration camps; and cutting off nearly all Boer supplies.

The starving Boer forces surrendered in May 1902. In addition to Mary Kingsley, many other well-known people served in the Boer War, including Mahatma Gandhi, Arthur Conan Doyle, and Winston Churchill.

Kingsley arrived, only one doctor and two other nurses. Many of the patients were suffering from typhoid fever and measles; others had been wounded while trying to escape prisoner-of-war camps and were slowly and painfully dying.

It was difficult and exhausting work. When Kingsley first arrived, she was able to spend her time off visiting Rudyard Kipling and his wife, who lived nearby. Kipling had traveled to South Africa to write about the war, and he greatly admired Kingsley, both for her brave accounts of her travels in West Africa and for her willingness to nurse in such a grim setting. She often had tea or supper with them, until their return to England in mid-April.

Kingsley attempted to write down some of what she had seen:

> When a man is dying definitely, you don't like the two next to turn to see the performance, so you trot off and find two little screens. Well, the other two know what those screens mean perfectly well; only they think they are there for them, so they start off on dying too. We have had four or five a night dying under these conditions since I was here on Sunday. Then there are the never-to-be-forgotten bugs and lice. They swarm.[73]

It was grim work, bloody, smelly, and dirty, and there was a constant risk of infection. By mid-May, Kingsley was fighting more than depression and exhaustion. She was, herself, fighting typhoid fever.

At first, she hid the symptoms from her coworkers, dealing with the headaches, fever, and dizziness as best she could. Gradually her symptoms grew worse. On June 1, Kingsley asked one of the other nurses to call the doctor. He quickly operated, and the surgery repaired her intestine, which had been perforated by the typhoid bacteria, but Kingsley remained weak.

Late on June 2, she called for the doctor. Kingsley knew that she was dying, and asked him to promise that her body would not be returned to England for burial in the family vault, but instead that she would be buried at sea, off the coast of her beloved Africa.

Mary Kingsley died early on the morning of June 3. She was 38 years old.

Rather than the simple burial at sea Kingsley had requested, she was instead given a military ceremony, since she was viewed as a war hero for her service. On the afternoon of June 4, her coffin, draped in the British flag, was ceremoniously taken to the pier, as a band played a somber funeral tune. Next, the coffin was placed on board the *H.M.S. Thrush*, which then steamed out to a point about three miles from the coast. After a brief ceremony, the flag was removed and the coffin lowered into the ocean.

The coffin had not been properly weighed down and, to the horror of those attending the ceremony; it did not sink, but floated off on the water, bobbing on top of the waves. A crew was dispatched in a small boat to retrieve the coffin; they then attached an anchor to it and it slowly sank.

Before Kingsley had left for South Africa, she had written to a friend a message that makes a fitting tribute to her life:

> Do not dream of in any way sacrificing yourself for any cause—I am not saying causes are not worth it but merely that they cannot be helped by sacrifice of that kind. Set yourself to gain personal power—don't grab the reins of power—but [while] they are laying on the horses neck, quietly get them into your hands and drive.[74]

Chronology

1862   Mary Kingsley is born on October 13, four days after her parents' wedding.

1866   Kingsley's younger brother, Charles, is born.

1879   Kingsley family moves to Kent; a neighbor begins to teach Kingsley engineering and science.

1884   Kingsley family moves to Cambridge. Berlin Conference begins on November 14.

1890   Kingsley's mother suffers a stroke.

1892   Kingsley's father and mother die.

1893   Kingsley makes first trip to Africa.

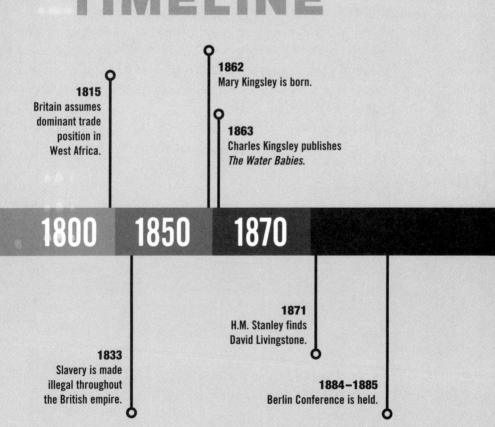

TIMELINE

1862
Mary Kingsley is born.

1815
Britain assumes dominant trade position in West Africa.

1863
Charles Kingsley publishes *The Water Babies*.

1800   **1850**   **1870**

1871
H.M. Stanley finds David Livingstone.

1833
Slavery is made illegal throughout the British empire.

1884–1885
Berlin Conference is held.

1894 Kingsley returns to England; begins work on *The Bights of Benin*. Departs for Africa on December 23.

1895 Kingsley travels through remote regions of Gabon, French Congo, and Cameroon.

1896 Kingsley becomes first white woman to climb Mount Cameroon. Returns to England in late November.

1897 *Travels in West Africa* is published.

1898 *West African Studies* is published.

1899 Kingsley leaves for South Africa to serve as a nurse in the Boer War. Dies on June 3 from typhoid fever.

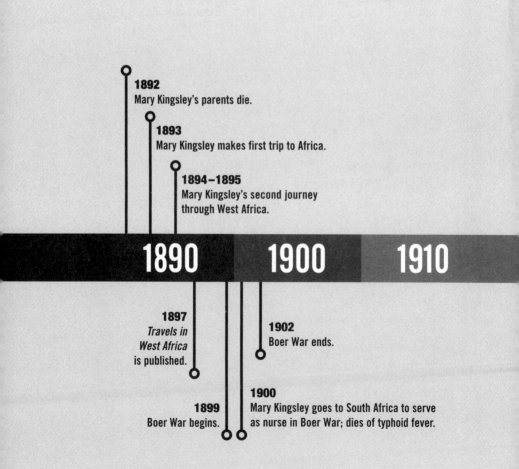

1892
Mary Kingsley's parents die.

1893
Mary Kingsley makes first trip to Africa.

1894–1895
Mary Kingsley's second journey through West Africa.

1890   **1900**   **1910**

1897
Travels in West Africa is published.

1902
Boer War ends.

1899
Boer War begins.

1900
Mary Kingsley goes to South Africa to serve as nurse in Boer War; dies of typhoid fever.

Notes

Chapter 1

1 Mary Kingsley, *Travels in West Africa*. Washington, D.C.: National Geographic, 2002, p. 1.

2 Katherine Frank, *A Voyager Out*. Boston: Houghton Mifflin, 1986, pp. 60–61.

3 Kingsley, *Travels in West Africa*, p. 4.

4 Ibid.

5 Ibid, p. 12.

6 Frank, *Voyager*, p. 70.

7 Kingsley, *Travels in West Africa*, p. 5.

8 Ibid, p. 9.

Chapter 2

9 Mary Kingsley, *Mainly About People* (1899), *ftp://spartacus.schoolnet.co.uk/Wkingsley.htm*.

10 Frank, *A Voyager Out*, p. 21.

11 Kingsley, *Mainly About People*.

12 National Portrait Gallery, *David Livingstone and the Victorian Encounter with Africa*, National Portrait Gallery, London, 1996, p. 116.

13 Mary Kingsley, "Life in West Africa," in *Women's Voices on Africa*, ed. Patricia W. Romero. Princeton: Markus Wiener Publishing, 1992, pp. 62–63.

Chapter 3

14 Mary Kingsley, *Notes on Sport and Travel* (1900), *ftp://www.spartacus.schoolnet.co.uk/Wkingsley.htm*.

15 Frank, *Voyager*, p. 35.

16 J. D. Fage, *A History of West Africa*. New York: Cambridge University Press, 1969, p. 165.

17 Frank, *Voyager*, p. 45.

18 Quoted in Alison Blunt, *Travel, Gender and Imperialism*. New York: Guilford Press, 1994, p. 48.

Chapter 4

19 Kingsley, *Travels in West Africa*, p. 1.

20 Blunt, *Travel, Gender and Imperialism*, pp. 68–69.

21 Anna Martin Hinderer, "Progress of the Work," in *Women's Voices on Africa*, pp. 37–39.

22 Fage, *A History of West Africa*, p. 64.

23 Ibid, p. 83.

24 Mary Kingsley, "Lembarene," *Women's Voices on Africa*, p. 57.

25 Fage, *A History of West Africa*, p. 131.

26 Anne Phillips, *The Enigma of Colonialism: British Policy in West Africa*. Bloomington: Indiana University Press, 1989, p. 158.

27 Mary Kingsley, "Life in West Africa," in *Women's Voices on Africa*, p. 70.

Chapter 5

28 Frank, *A Voyager Out*, p. 90.

29 Ibid.

30 Blunt, *Travel, Gender and Imperialism*, p. 53.

31 Kingsley, *Travels in West Africa*, p. 10.

32 Frank, *A Voyager Out*, p. 110.

33 Kingsley, *Travels in West Africa*, p. 18.

34 Ibid, p. 30.

35 Frank, *A Voyager Out*, pp. 125–126.

36 Ibid, p. 128.

Chapter 6

37 Joseph Conrad, *Heart of Darkness*, (New York: W.W. Norton, 1988), p. 16.

38 Kingsley, *Travels in West Africa*, p. 65.

39 Ibid.

40 Ibid, pp. 70–71.

41 Ibid, p. 87

42 Ibid.

43 Ibid, p. 88.

44 Ibid, p. 93.

45 Ibid, p. 96.

46 Frank, *A Voyager Out*, p. 154.

47 Ibid, p. 161.

48 Ibid.

49 Kingsley, *Travels in West Africa*, p. 113.

50 Ibid, p. 119.

51 Ibid, p. 120

52 Ibid, p. 123.

53 Frank, *A Voyager Out*, p. 162.

Chapter 7

54 Kingsley, "Life in West Africa," in *Women's Voices on Africa*, p. 64.

55 Kingsley, *Travels in West Africa*, p. 137.

56 Ibid, p. 141.

57 Ibid, p. 147.

58 Ibid, p. 149.

59 Ibid, p. 152

60 Ibid, p. 159.

61 Ibid, p. 167.

62 Ibid, p. 170.

63 Ibid, p. 228.

64 Frank, *A Voyager Out*, p. 188.

65 Kingsley, *Travels in West Africa*, p. 321.

66 Ibid, p. 330.

67 Ibid, p. 355.

68 Ibid, p. 365.

Chapter 8

69 Blunt, *Travel, Gender and Imperialism*, p. 116.

70 Ibid.

71 Frank, *A Voyager Out*, p. 239.

72 Ibid, p. 272.

73 Ibid, p. 293.

74. Blunt, *Travel, Gender and Imperialism*, p. 127.

Bibliography

Books

Alexander, Caroline. *One Dry Season: In the Footsteps of Mary Kingsley.* New York: Vintage Books, 1989.

Blunt, Alison. *Travel, Gender, and Imperialism: Mary Kingsley and West Africa.* New York: Guilford Press, 1994.

Carnes, J. A. *Journal of a Voyage from Boston to the West Coast of Africa.* New York: Negro University Press, 1969.

Conrad, Joseph. *Heart of Darkness.* New York: W. W. Norton , 1988.

Crowe, S. E. *The Berlin West African Conference, 1884–1885.* London: Longmans, Green, 1942.

Fage, J. D. *A History of West Africa.* New York: Cambridge University Press, 1969.

Frank, Katherine. *A Voyager Out: The Life of Mary Kingsley.* Boston: Houghton Mifflin, 1986.

Greene, Graham. *Journey Without Maps.* New York: Penguin Books, 1936.

Huxley, Elspeth. *Four Guineas: A Journey Through West Africa.* London: Chatto and Windus, 1957.

Kingsley, Mary. *Travels in West Africa.* Washington, D.C.: National Geographic, 2002.

Lewis, Ethelreda. *Trader Horn.* New York: Simon and Schuster, 1927.

Macmillan, Allister, ed. *The Red Book of West Africa.* London: Frank Cass, 1968.

Moore, Decima and F. G. Guggisberg. *We Two in West Africa.* New York: Charles Scribner's Sons, 1909.

National Portrait Gallery. *David Livingstone and the Victorian Encounter with Africa.* London: National Portrait Gallery, 1996.

Oliver, Caroline. *Western Women in Colonial Africa.* Westport, CT: Greenwood Press, 1982.

Phillips, Anne. *The Enigma of Colonialism: British Policy in West Africa.* Bloomington: Indiana University Press, 1989.

Romero, Patricia W., ed. *Women's Voices on Africa.* Princeton: Markus Wiener Publishing, 1992.

Stanley, Richard and Neame, Alan, eds. *The Exploration Diaries of H.M. Stanley.* London: William Kimber, 1961.

....

Websites
Anglo Boer War Museum
http://www.anglo-boer.co.za

The Boer War
http://www.geocities.com/athens/acropolis/8141/boerwar/

Century Library
http://www.dundeecity.gov.uk/centlib/slessor/

Cornell: Department of Neurobiology and Behavior
http://www.nbb.cornell.edu/neurobio/

Guardian Unlimited: 1899–1909
http://www.guardiancentury.co.uk/1899-1909/

International Albert Schweitzer Foundation
http://www.schweitzer.org

Missionary Biographies: Mary Slessor
http://www.wholesomewords.org/missions/bioslessor2.html

Taffnet—HM Stanley
http://www.cyberphile.co.uk/~taff/taffnet/pages/stanley.htm

Further Reading

Books

Bryson, Bill. *My African Diary*. New York: Broadway Books, 2002.

Dugard, Martin. *Into Africa: The Epic Adventures of Stanley and Livingstone*. New York: Doubleday and Company, 2003.

Greene, Graham. *Journey Without Maps*. New York: Penguin, 1977.

Polk, Milbry and Tiegreen, Mary. *Women of Discovery*. New York: Clarkson Potter, 2001.

Roberts, David, ed. *Points Unknown: A Century of Great Exploration*. New York: W. W. Norton , 2000.

Shaffer, Tanya. *Somebody's Heart is Burning: A Woman Wanderer in Africa*. New York: Vintage Books, 2003.

Whybrow, Helen, ed. *Dead Reckoning: Great Adventure Writing from the Golden Age of Exploration, 1800–1900*. New York: W. W. Norton, 2002.

Websites

Enchanted Learning: Zoom Explorers
http://www.enchantedlearning.com/explorers

Living on Earth
http://www.loe.org/series/discovery_women/kingsley

Mary Henrietta Kingsley
http://www.nbb.cornell.edu/neurobio/hopkins/MKHrefs.html

Mary Kingsley
http://www.spartacus.schoolnet.co.uk/Wkingsley.htm

Victorian Web
http://www.victorianweb.org

Index

Index

Kondo Kondo, Mary landing on in second trip to West Africa, 64

Lambaréné, Mary in on second trip to West Africa, 57–60
Lander, Richard, 38
lectures, Mary delivering, 44, 69, 85–86, 87
Leopold II, 27
Liberia
    freed slaves in, 37–38, 39
    as independent republic, 38, 40
    missionaries in, 39
    and United States, 37–38, 39
Libreville, French Congo, Mary in on second trip to West Africa, 55, 79
lice, and Mary's second trip to West Africa, 73
lilies, Mary collecting on second trip to West Africa, 64
Livingstone, David, 2, 17, 18, 20, 33
Lockyer, Norman, 17

MacDonald, Lady, 45, 46–47, 48–49, 50, 51–53
MacDonald, Sir Claude, 45, 49, 50, 51
Macmillan, George (publisher), 43, 46, 85
malaria, Mary suffering from, 67, 69, 70
manioc, as native diet, 65–66
M'bo, 62, 63
meat, as native diet, 66
Mediterranean, Mary's father traveling in, 12, 14
Mission Evangelique, in Lambaréné, 60, 64, 65

missionaries
    Mary's view of, 39
    in West Africa, 20, 33–34, 38–40, 47–48, 55, 60, 61, 64, 65, 66, 78, 79–80, 81
Monrovia, Liberia, 37–38
mosquitoes, and Mary's second trip to West Africa, 57–59, 70, 73
Mové (boat), 55–57
Murray, John, 46

National History Museum (Kensington, England), 64
Ncovi, Lake, Mary on in second trip to West Africa, 71, 72
Netherlands, and trade with West Africa, 35, 36
New Mexico, Mary's father traveling in, 25
New Zealand, Mary's father traveling in, 25
Ngouta, 65
Niger (boat), 79
Niger Coast Protectorate, and Great Britain, 45
Niger River
    and Berlin Conference, 27, 28
    British control of, 45
    exploration of, 38
Nigeria
    as British colony, 39
    missionaries in, 39
Nile River, exploration of, 17
Njole, Mary in on second trip to West Africa, 61–62, 64–65
Norfolk, Duke of, 12
North Africa, Mary's father traveling in, 12
Notes on Sport and Travel (book), 44

Index

Index

Picture Credits

Cover: © Hulton|Archive by Getty Images

Contributors

Heather Lehr Wagner is a writer and editor. She earned an MA in government from the College of William and Mary and a BA in political science from Duke University. She has written more than 20 books, including biographies and studies of global points of conflict, and authored *Gertrude Bell* in the Women Explorers series.

Series consulting editor **Milbry Polk** graduated from Harvard in 1976. An explorer all her life, she has ridden horseback through Pakistan's Northwest Territories, traveled with Bedouin tribesmen in Jordan and Egypt, surveyed Arthurian sites in Wales, and trained for the first Chinese-American canoe expedition. In 1979, supported by the National Geographic Society, Polk led a camel expedition retracing the route of Alexander the Great across Egypt.

Her work as a photojournalist has appeared in numerous magazines, including *Time, Fortune, Cosmopolitan* and *Quest*. Currently she is a contributing editor to the *Explorers Journal*. Polk is a Fellow of the Royal Geographic Society and a Fellow of the Explorers Club. She is the also the author of two award-winning books, *Egyptian Mummies* (Dutton Penguin, 1997) and *Women of Discovery* (Clarkson Potter, 2001).

Milbry Polk serves as an advisor to the George Polk Awards for Journalistic Excellence, is on the Council of the New York Hall of Science, serves on the Board of Governors of the National Arts Club, the Children's Shakespeare Theater Board and is the director of Wings World Quest. She lives in Palisades, New York, with her husband and her three daughters. She and her daughters row on the Hudson River.